FROM ANNA + MATT on m~ ~

BIRTH DAY. 6/23/1~

MY PADUCAH

From the Early Years to the Present

by

Barron White

In association with

McClanahan
Publishing House

Cover design and book layout by James Asher Graphics

Manufactured in the United States of America

All book order correspondence should be addressed to:

Barrons Books
4704 Buckner Lane
Paducah, KY 42001-5352

270-443-1205

bwhitey@webtv.net

In association with

McClanahan
Publishing House

DEDICATION

This book is dedicated to my wife, Zelma,
and to our daughters,
Kathy White, Smyrna, Georgia,
and Liz White Hansen, Waynesville, Ohio.

ACKNOWLEDGEMENTS

Like any endeavor that covers many subjects and areas, this book has been written with the support of many people. There is a need to give special thanks to some friends who made contributions vital to completing this book: Sam Boaz, Beverly McKinley, Monroe Sloan, P.J. Grumley, Eugene Katterjohn, Elmer Breidert, Emmett Holt, Walter "Dub" Beasley, Jimmelyn Huston, Katherne Flowers, Pat Tubbs, Violet Starr Cummins, Dr. Gene E. Paro of Huntsville, Alabama, Tom Terrell of Miami, Florida, John Iler of Arlington, Virginia, and Harry Smith of Boulder City, Nevada.

And special thanks to Gay Baker, editor, Paula Cunningham, publisher, and Jim Asher, design artist.

And very special thanks to my dear wife, Zelma, whose loving patience, tolerance and support have been invaluable. She reviewed every story, took e-mails and phone calls, offered criticisms and suggestions, and helped by making trips and deliveries for and with me. Also most grateful thanks to daughters Kathy and Liz, who although very busy with their own lives away from here, were always most generous with their help in guiding me through the maze and intricacies of computer land as they coached me step by step though the mysteries of copying, scanning, and downloading.

I would be remiss if I failed to acknowledge the many letters and responses from so many friends old and new who have written to tell me how much they enjoyed my book, "I Remember Paducah When," published in 2000. Their encouragement and expressed appreciation have been the impetus for this book.

CONTENTS

Tony Janus, Pilot; Roy Hoewisher, "Santa Claus"-Paducah Riverfront 1913

PADUCAH BEFORE 1923

Most of the stories in my book, *"I Remember Paducah When,"* published November 2000, and in this one, are concerned with people and places I knew from personal experience from 1923 to the present. But Paducah history from its earliest days has always been of interest to me. Having had free time since retirement in 1989, I have been researching older records. Newspapers contain a lot of wonderful stories about events that deserve to be saved, but it would be impossible to save and store the mountains of newsprint. Each day's issue soon becomes history and sinks further and further into the past. But thankfully, microfilm copies are available for anyone who has the time and inclination to laboriously wade through them. Watching page after page of print move across the small screen by the hour will make you cross-eyed, but the rewards of finding "sunken treasure" make it all worthwhile.

Some years ago, my good friend G. Anthony "Tony" Johnston, fellow Rotarian and former Scout leader, showed me a picture of a "flying boat" that visited Paducah in the early 1900s. Recently, while serving on the Paducah Chamber of Commerce Business Evolution Committee to collect photographs of old Paducah scenes and buildings, I recalled the old picture of the plane on the riverfront. I contacted Johnston's daughter, Tona, now a resident of Frankfort, Kentucky, who very graciously sent me a copy. At the bottom was printed, "Arrival of Santa Claus in his Hydro-Aeroplane for Rudy's (department store)-December 13." On the back was written, "Dec.13, 1913 -Tony Janus-Aviator, Roy Hoewischer-Santa Claus."

After learning the exact date this plane was here, I scanned microfilm of old newspapers on file at the Paducah Library and found an article dated December 6, 1913, which read, "Tony Janus, the man of the winds, who thrilled Paducah last May during the Home Coming, arrived in Paducah with a proposition which he presented to a committee representing Paducah, and if the proposal is accepted, Janus will come next week for three weeks in his flying boat in which he has been giving exhibitions at Cairo since Thanksgiving."

This sent me to the May film, which indicated that Janus came to Paducah May 19, during one of Paducah's big events. In 1913 Home-coming Week was held from May 19 to 24, with a street fair each day and parades at night. The main attraction was "Chief Paduke's" triumphant return to Paducah, with the Chief impersonated by Attorney James C. Wheeler mounted on a white horse. The newspapers were filled with stories and pictures of each day's events, which were witnessed by fifteen thousand people who thronged the streets at Fifth and Broadway.

One of the best records of this occasion was in Fred Neuman's 1927 book, "The Story of Paducah." He covered the week's activities nicely in his three-page summary, which included the information that a pilot "in his airplane winged his way across the Ohio River and over the city each afternoon." To me, the fact that the first airplane of record visited Paducah was a story that should rank equally in importance with Chief Paduke's return. After all, the Wright Brothers had made the first flight only 10 years before.

Newspaper reports on microfilm said that when Janus' plane arrived that afternoon, he had it assembled on the levee at the foot of Kentucky Avenue by mechanics J.W. Smith and W.O. Ingalls. He began making flights at 10 a.m. and 2 p.m. Several thousand people lined the wharf on the morning of the first flight, which was billed as the first flight ever in Paducah for a hydroplane. He attained a height of 500 feet, flew for 14 minutes, circled Owen's Island, and flew up and down the river. On his second flight, Colonel Ben Weille was taken along as a passenger. The charge was $35 for a flight. Bad weather kept him from flying some mornings. With the wind at his back, he could attain a speed of 85 miles per hour. While he was there for the week, he usually "pursued a course of downstream, circling and dipping, and returning, making a play for the thousands on the levee, darting back and forth across the water and finally making a perfect landing."

On Thursday, December 22, for the first time, he left the course of the river, and made a swing over the business district, coming as far west as Third Street. After returning to the river, he made a number of evolutions on the surface of the water and exhibited "splendid control of the machine." The next day, the last of his engagement, a large crowd was on hand to witness his departure.

The newspapers carried a feature story on the front page every day about "birdman" Tony Janus, who thrilled the crowds with flights each day in his Benoist hydro-aeroplane. The May 24 paper reported, "Daring aviator Tony Janus will fly back to St. Louis, making only one stop at Cape Girardeau on the 250-mile trip, which would take six hours." The next day's paper headline read, "JANUS MAKES SPLENDID TIME - RETURNS SAFELY."

EARLY MEMORIES

KINFOLKS

In 1923 when the White family boarded the Illinois Central train in Memphis and came here to live, we children had never heard of Paducah. We knew no one here. We knew that we would be meeting people new to us. One of our first impressions was that most people here had been born here and were all kin to one another. We became acquainted with the Langstaffs when we moved into their upstairs apartment on Kentucky Avenue. Their family had moved here in the 1850s and they had kinfolk scattered all over town. A neighbor, Carrie Rieke, was a member of an old-time family and also had many relatives here. The Hanks, Kolbs, Nagels, and Runges were and still are related. After going through school here, working downtown for over fifty years, being involved with many civic, social and business organizations, it was as if I had lived here always. When I would tell people on our bus tours that I was not a native, having lived here for ONLY the last seventy years, that always got a few chuckles.

One of the first families I met was the Fowlers. My father had opened his first grocery at 621 Broadway in a building owned by Mrs. Saunders Fowler, who lived at 801 Broadway. Their son Gus, just out of high school, worked in Dad's store before going off to college. The old Fowler home at 619 Kentucky Avenue was still the residence of Martha Fowler and her sister Josephine Fowler Post, daughters of Captain Joe Fowler, who died in 1904. Joe and his four brothers, Dick, Gus, Will and White, had operated steamboats on the Ohio and Tennessee rivers since the mid-1800s. Their father, Judge Wiley P. Fowler, had settled in Smithland as a small boy after he landed at the mouth of Island Creek in 1817.

It was not until my retirement years that I made a search of our family history. Pat Tubbs, (Mrs. Russell Tubbs), a wonderful young woman who worked with me at Petter Supply Company, was interested in her family history and helped me discover my great-grandparents, who had lived and died in West Tennessee after having come from North Carolina in the 1800s. One search she made for me was a record of great-grandfather John Worthan White, who first married Lacy Fowler, then when she died, married her sister Louisa. It did not occur to me that there might be kinship between the Tennessee and Kentucky Fowlers and I never thought to investigate.

In June of 2000, while reviewing microfilm at the Paducah Public Library, I discovered a film entitled "The Annals of the Fowler Family." I had done quite a bit of research in other records of the Fowlers and had written and given several talks about them. But since this film contained several hundred pages, I knew there would be much more information than I had previously located. As I scanned through the pages, I came upon one that was headed "CHILDREN OF LACY (FOWLER) AND JOHN WORTHAN WHITE OF TENNESSEE." Hey! I thought, "That's my great-grandfather." And in fact, as I read further for several pages, I discovered that the Paducah White and Fowler families are related. So now I have a deeper feeling of closeness and kinship for my town of Paducah, Kentucky, a place that I have learned to love.

THE FOWLER FAMILY HISTORY

M any of the Fowler family members in Paducah are descendants of Judge Wiley P. Fowler. He was born Sept 2, 1799 in Smith County, Tennessee, was raised on a farm, left home in 1819, moved to Arkansas and farmed there until about 1822. He studied law and was admitted to practice in 1823. He set up practice in the Jackson Purchase and settled in Salem, which was then the Livingston County seat. Salem at that time had a population of 250, with a little fewer than 6,000 in the county. Smithland had a population of about 400, and was the largest settlement in the extreme western section of Kentucky. Columbus had approximately 220, Paducah 100, and Mayfield fewer than 50.

Judge Fowler married Miss Esther Araminta Given and they were the parents of five children, including Gus and Joe H. Fowler, who became riverboat captains and operators. After the death of his second wife in 1877, Judge Fowler came to Paducah to live with his son, Capt. Joe H. Fowler, who was the only one of his sons to outlive him. Judge Fowler died in 1880 and was buried in Smithland Cemetery.

In 1850, Joe had become interested in the wharfboat and steamboat business. He became a clerk on the Paducah-Nashville packet "Annie Linington" and after seven years received his master's license. Later he got into the boat and boat store business in Paducah. With his brother Gus, he had an interest in the "Gus Fowler" packet boat, which operated on the Ohio River. In 1855, Joe married Miss Mattie Leech of Smithland. They had five children: Given, Mildred Davis, Mrs. Cook Husbands, Josephine Post and Mattie. Joe's brothers, Dick, Will, Gus and White Fowler preceded him in death.

During the heyday of the river packet steamboat from 1870 to 1910, the Fowler brothers' boats were among the fastest and best known on the rivers. The Fowlers had joined with John Gilbert and the Evansville, Cairo and Memphis Steam Company to create the Paducah and Cairo Packet Company, offering a packet service on the Ohio and Mississippi rivers. Their boat, "Joe Fowler," ran from Paducah to Evansville and the steamer "Dick Fowler" ran from Paducah to Cairo. By 1895 and after seven years as a U.S. mail carrier, the "Joe Fowler" had traveled 327,000 miles and had carried 152,400 passengers without a single loss of life. While not connected directly as captain on some boats, Joe held a master's license and was associated in many ways with a large number of packet boats including: "Idlewild," "Sam Orr," "Armanda," "Silver Cloud," "Red Cloud," "Gus Fowler," "Dick Fowler," "Joe Fowler," "John Gilbert," and several others.

Joe became president of the Fowler-Crumbaugh Boat Store at First and Broadway and spent most of the last years of his life there. He served several terms on the city council and on the city board of education. Three of his brothers served in the Confederate Army during the Civil War. Joe was never a soldier, but with stubborn loyalty to the Confederacy, he defied the Union officers stationed in Paducah. When General Forrest and his men attacked Fort Anderson, the wharfboat was loaded with citizens fleeing for their lives, and while Federal gunboats patrolled the riverfront shelling the town, Captain Fowler transported his boat and all the passengers to safety on the Illinois shore. Captain Joe died December 4, 1904 and is buried in the Fowler family plot in Oak Grove Cemetery. A large stone obelisk marks his grave.

Captain Joe's only son, Given, became the clerk at the boat store as a young man and held that position for twelve years. Later he became master of the packet boat "Dick Fowler" and others for the rest of his life. Given died in 1921.

As most of my adult working life was spent near the river and being involved with the marine trade, I soon developed a keen interest in Paducah history and the impact the rivers had on the city's development. Since the Fowler family had been a big part of the river industry, I decided after retirement that I would research their history.

In 1926, I became aware of the Fowler family, when we moved into the three-story frame McCall house at 626 Kentucky Ave. Today the location houses the offices of Charles R. Moffitt, CPA, who remodeled the former Claude Baker Oldsmobile agency building on that site. Our house was across the street from the well-known Joe Fowler home place. Captain Joe Henry Fowler had built the home during the time that he owned and operated paddlewheel steamboats and the Paducah Wharfboat on the Ohio River. Two of his daughters, Josephine Fowler Post, a widow, and Mattie, who never married, still lived in the old home, which had been the head-quarters for Colonel Stephan C. Hicks of the Union Army during his stay in Paducah during the Civil War. His granddaughter, Martha Davis Bringhurst, lived next door to us. Her daughter, Mildred Bringhurst, was my classmate in high school. Martha Bringhurst's sister-in-law, Marjorie Fowler Davis, and son Frank Fowler Davis, lived in the old Lloyd Tilghman home on the corner of 7th and Kentucky. We saw Frank and his mother frequently during the period before World War II, as his mother owned and operated an auto garage and gas station on the northwest corner of 4th and Kentucky. Frank was very proud of his family heritage and always introduced himself to others as Frank FOWLER Davis. I last saw Frank when we were both stationed at Jefferson Barracks in St. Louis during WWII. We were both in the Air Force, but in different units.

JOSEPHINE FOWLER POST

One of Joe Fowler's daughters, Mrs. Josephine Fowler Post, is probably the best remembered by Paducahans, as she lived at the old family home at 619 Kentucky Avenue until her death in September 1946. She was graduated from Miss Florence Hines private school in Paducah in 1867. In 1892 she married Edmund Morrow Post, who died in 1900. They had one son, Joe Fowler Post, who died in 1910.

Mrs. Post was a staunch supporter of the women's suffrage movement, the Women's Christian Temperance Union, and was active in her church. She took an active interest in several campaigns of the Democratic party and was regarded as one of the most influential women in Paducah. Her prominence as a speaker on patriotic and women's suffrage topics gained national attention and she was called to Washington, D.C., to serve on the National Staff of the Women's Suffrage Association. She was appointed by the governor of Kentucky to represent the state in the centennial of Thomas

Jefferson in 1926 at Monticello and the University of Virginia. She was a member of the Kentucky Museum Commission, and the Paducah Museum Committee and was ex-regent and vice-regent of the Paducah chapter of the DAR and the UDC. She was president of the Delphic Club, a member of the Women's Club and the National Garden Club of America. For 25 years she taught a bible class at the Broadway Methodist Church. The National Federation of Women's Clubs presented her with a medal as "The Pioneer Club Woman" in 1940 and she was a guest in the White House in 1941 when Mrs. Chapman Catt, the women's suffrage leader, was presented a medal by the Chi Omega Association.

Mrs. Post died in 1946 at age 76 and is buried in Oak Grove Cemetery in the Fowler family plot. When we lived across the street at 626 Kentucky Ave. in 1926-1928, we visited in the Fowler home many times and were told by the two sisters to make generous use of their grape arbor in the big garden between their house and the James Rudy home, which we did frequently.

JOE ROETTEIS, JR.

An article in the Paducah News-Democrat March 4, 1964 carried the headline, "JOSEPH ROETTEIS, WORLD WAR I HERO, DIES AT 73." At this time, very few people living in Paducah ever knew or heard of this man, who was reported to be the most decorated World War I soldier from this area.

The Roetteis family came to this country from France in 1865. Joe's maternal great-grandfather, Hippolite Victor Pichon of Marners, France, came to Paducah at the age of 20 and married Pauline Euphrasine Marie Drouet in Paducah on August 29, 1869. He purchased farmland on the north side of Paducah and became a truck gardener like his father, Jean Louis Pichon in France. Hippolite's daughter Virginia married Laurence Joseph Roetteis, (Joe's father) on April 12, 1887. He was born December 25, 1861 in Les Bourg, France, and came to America at about the age of 21.

Joseph Roetteis-Most Decorated World War I Soldier in McCracken County-Joseph Roetteis was a World War I hero and recipient of the Croix de Guerre, the highest French medal honoring fighting men. Mr. Roetteis, who died in 1964, served in the U.S. Marine Corps from 1917 through 1919, also receiving the Fleur de Guerre (a regimental citation) and five bronze stars while serving as a machine gunner and ammunition carrier through some of the bloodiest battles of World War I, including Verdun.

When he and Virginia Ann married, he received a wedding gift of ten acres of farmland on the south side of town, which he developed into a truck farm. Although their farm was productive, it was also very hard work for both of them and Virginia died young at age 49. They had ten children; nine lived to marry and have families of their own. A few of their descendants still live in the Paducah area.

Joseph Roetteis, Jr. was born March 31, 1890. Around the turn of the century the family moved to a home on the south side of Mill Street, just off Powell in the Mechanicsburg area. Joe and several of his brothers - Clarence, Louis, and Frank - were working at the Paducah Cooperage Company, out on Meyers Street on the bank of the Tennessee River. Joe and his other brothers also helped their father on the farm and at the Market House on Second Street between Broadway and Kentucky Avenue, where their father operated a stall for many years.

In 1917 at the age of 27, Joe Jr. volunteered for the U.S. Navy and joined the U.S. Marines, was assigned to the Headquarters Detachment 6th Machine Gun Battalion, and served as a machine gunner and ammunitions carrier through some of the bloodiest battles of the war, including Verdun through the last battle in the Argonne Forest. For his action he was awarded the Croix de Guerre, the highest French medal honoring fighting men. He also received the French Fleur de Guerre (a regimental citation), five Bronze Stars and several other general citations. He was wounded twice and was discharged in 1919.

Upon his return to Paducah, Joe worked as an automobile mechanic and lived with his parents on Mill Street. He soon married Fay Paxton, whose sister Fern had married his brother William. Joe and Fay bought a home on Minnich, where they lived the rest of their lives. Joe accepted a job as a machinist at the F.K. Pence tile works on North 7th Street. After a few years, he worked for the Shelton Bros. Machine Shop on South 3rd Street, operated by Fred and Russell Shelton. In 1947 he began working at the Ellis Bros. Machine Shop on Broadway between First and Second streets. Fay, who suffered for many years with arthritis, died January 3, 1948. Joe continued as a machinist at Ellis Bros. until shortly before his death in March 1964. He was buried in Maplelawn Cemetery with full military honors by members of the Disabled American Veterans.

My first memory of Joe and Fay was sometime in 1935, when they joined the First Church Of Christ, Scientist at 14th and Broadway, where my family had been members since coming to Paducah. After my graduation from high school in 1931, the church board assigned me to the usher committee, where I served until I left for the Army in 1942. During that time I would greet Mr. and Mrs. Roetteis every Sunday as they arrived in their vintage auto a few minutes before the start of the service. Joe was in his mid-forties then, slight of build, always neatly dressed; always wearing a gray soft cap. Fay Paxton Roetteis, a few years younger, was pretty, petite, and very slender. Arthritis had crippled her early in their marriage and Joe was always by her side helping her get around, up stairs and in and out of their car. Joe was a very kind, gentle man, reserved and quiet, but very warm and friendly to everyone.

My mother, then a widow, and I made many visits to their home and small orchard on Minnich Avenue, which in those times was considered "out in the country." Their home was neat and spotless, and the orchard was always well kept. Joe loved flowers and spent most of his leisure time outdoors, planting, pruning and trimming. Being a mechanic, he always had everything in good working order. During mild and pretty weather, he would assist Fay to one of several places where she could sit, rest and watch him in their back yard. Joe, a very modest and unassuming man, would never mention his wartime experience, but would freely speak about it if asked.

In 1947, he went to work for the Ellis machine shop. Since this was just around the corner from my First Street office at Petter, I would see him almost daily as I went to and fro morning, noon and night. When Fay died in 1948, he continued to live on Minnich and to work at the machine shop until shortly before his death in 1964 at age 73.

REAR ADMIRAL JOE COOK CLIFTON

Most Paducahans know that Joe Clifton Drive is North 28th Street between Broadway and Park Avenue. But it is unlikely that many people know just who Joe Clifton was. Rear Admiral Joe Cook Clifton was a highly decorated World War II combat pilot and career Navy officer who was enshrined into the National Museum of Naval Aviation Hall of Fame in May of 1996. Joe, who died in 1967, was one of the most colorful and well-loved Naval personalities of his day. His nickname was "Jumping Joe." He logged more than 10,000 hours in propeller and jet aircraft. His group inflicted this damage on the Japanese: 102 planes destroyed, 78 planes damaged, 104,500 tons of shipping sunk and 198,500 tons of shipping damaged. His decorations included the Legion of Merit with Gold Star, the Distinguished Flying Cross with Gold Star, two Air Medals and the DSO (Distinguished Service Order) of Great Britain.

I became aware of Joe Clifton when after a week of perfect attendance at grade school, I was one of those given a free ticket to the week's football game at Tilghman High School. For the first two weeks of the season, I had no interest in football and didn't use my ticket. Luke Nichol, a boy my age who lived on Broadway and whose house backed up to ours, went to St. Mary's Academy and every week he came to my house asking for my ticket, which I gave him. Then I began to hear of the exploits of a football star at the high school named Joe Clifton, so I decided to use the tickets from then on.

In 1925, his senior year of high school, Joe was elected class president. He attended the University of Kentucky, but left for the Naval Academy at Annapolis, where he was a star fullback on the football team and was twice named an All-American. He was graduated in 1930 and earned his wings in 1932. He commanded fighter squadrons and air groups during World War II. While flying from the carrier "Saratoga," Joe shot down five Japanese aircraft, earning the flying designation of "ace." He is best remembered for his leadership, especially during the 1943 air strike at Raboul, a highly fortified harbor of New Guinea and for his command of the combined American-British force in air strikes against Japanese-held territory in Sumatra. In 1945 he served two years as commander of the carrier "Wasp." In 1949, he held a command at Rhein-Main, Germany, leading other squadrons during Operation "Vittles," the Berlin Air Lift.

For several years, he commanded the Naval air training station in Memphis, Tennessee, and between 1956 and his retirement seven years later; he held a number of other command posts. He retired from active Naval service in 1963, having served for 37 years. Joe then joined Litton Industries, where he became director for guidance and controls systems. He died in 1967 at the age of 59 and was buried with full military honors in Arlington National Cemetery. Although he received some of the highest awards, Joe never lost his down-home touch and would occasionally fly home to visit his mother Pearl, who lived at 1309 Jefferson Street. It has been rumored that some of his squad members said that Joe would quote

Joe Clifton was a highly decorated combat pilot during World War II.

Bible passages while enroute to targets in the Pacific, in order to keep up their spirits. If this is true, it was probably a result of his early religious training. His mother was a member of the First Church of Christ, Scientist at 14th and Broadway. Joe seldom attended church, but I understand that he attended Sunday school.

Many of Clifton's written documents and uniforms are housed in the Market House Museum at Second and Broadway.

ADMIRAL EUGENE E. PARO

Gene Paro was born in Paducah on February 22,1904. His parents were Edward S. and Lazetta (Zetta) Paro, who lived at 328 Harahan Boulevard, in the home of her parents, Henry T. and Mary Maffet. His father and grandfather were engineers for the Illinois Central Railroad. His father was killed in a train wreck when Gene was three. Gene entered Washington High School in 1916, and was a member of the fourteen-man football squad the year Paducah won the West Kentucky football championship. Home games were played on Wilhelm Field, located on the west side of the school. Gene was the fullback on the 1919 team and scored the only Paducah touchdown when Mayfield beat them 85-6. He was a member of the basketball team and in his senior year was assistant editor of the "Owaissa," the high school annual. He graduated in 1920. At that time the high school was on Broadway between Twelfth and Thirteenth streets. When Augusta Tilghman was built on Murrell Boulevard in 1921, Washington High became Washington Junior High School.

Paro was a graduate of the U.S. Naval Academy in 1925, and spent most of his career in the Far East, commanding submarines, destroyer escort divisions, and serving on the staff of General S.B. Buckner Jr.'s. 10th Army during the planning and assault on Okinawa in World War II. His decorations included the Silver Star, Purple Heart, and a Presidential Citation. Having been raised on Harahan Boulevard, he wrote of his early days in his biography, "To Catch a Crawdad," a delightful story of his visits to the Market House, Paducah's first airplane, the flood of 1910, circuses, and railroads. A limited number of copies were printed, but were never published for the general public to read.

When he retired from the Navy, he returned to Paducah with his wife, Nancy, and moved into the family home on the Lovelaceville Road, that he inherited from his mother, Zetta Paro Burnham. The property had been called "Landfall Farm" and had an interesting history. The house was built in the 1880s and the original owner of the property was Moses Morrow, who received a grant of 425 acres from the State of Kentucky in 1825. When he died around 1850, his son William, a slave owner, inherited the property. According to deed book records, one of William Morrow's heirs, Mary Ellen Morrow, received the property as part of her allotment, and she sold the property in the early 1900s. Gene's mother acquired the tract and house in 1930 and was the owner until her death in 1944, when Admiral Paro inherited it. In 1952 he decided to move the house up the hill behind the old site to the corner of Gum Springs Road.

Paro, who had been described as an artist, an inventor, an engineer, and a writer, became very visible in town. He made a second career in the fine arts field. He studied at fine art academies in

Admiral Eugene E.
Paro (U.S. Navy)
1904-1990

Philadelphia, Paris, Manila and Rome. Many of his works were created at his home in Paducah. In 1960 Paro served on a committee to help obtain TVA power for Paducah. The names of those who served were unknown to any-one but themselves. Besides Paro, the members included Dick Fairhurst, Joe Mitchell, John Oehlschlaeger, Henry Whitlow and Ed Paxton. In order that their opposition would not sabotage their plans, they decided to meet in secret. They selected the Paro home for their meetings, since it was remote enough to avoid suspicion. Joe Mitchell did the advertising and promotion to educate the public. Clyde Boyles was finance chairman and raised $30,000. Paducah won the election for TVA power on November 6, 1960.

Admiral Paro took a position with McGraw Construction Company in Korea during that war. He and Nancy lived at Landfall Farm from 1950 until her death in 1987. Paro continued to live there a few years until his son Gene Jr. moved his dad to his home in Alabama, where he died in 1990. Gene and Nancy are buried in Arlington National Cemetery.

I became personally aware of Admiral Gene Paro around

1960. He would occasionally accompany his wife Nancy to Sunday services at the First Church of Christ, Scientist, where I was a member and head usher. He would park his car on Broadway west of the 14th Street intersection and stride back to the church front entrance on the corner of 14th Street with Nancy at his side. He usually wore a dark felt hat with a wide brim, and carried either a cane or what looked like a "swagger" stick. His visage was serious and authoritative. He would blink an acknowledgment to my greeting and find a place near the back. His demeanor was pleasant, but slightly intimidating and did not invite conversation. Nancy was warm and friendly and he would wait patiently for her while she chatted a moment with members.

His mother's home at 328 Harahan was two doors north of our home at 316 Harahan. She was living there during the three short years that we were there in the late 1920s, but I don't recall seeing him in the neighborhood. When our family used the Petter company cabin on Sledd Creek at Kentucky Lake on weekends once every year, we understood that the Paros frequently stayed at his brother Edward's large cabin a short distance away out on a slim finger on the lake, overlooking the dam.

After an extended search, I was able to locate Gene's son, Dr. Gene E. Paro, now living in Huntsville, Alabama. He also has an impressive record. He graduated from the U.S. Naval Academy in 1951 and was first in his class of 923 in physical fitness. He won athletic awards in football, boxing, and basketball. He served 24 years in the U.S. Marine Corps, retiring in 1977 with the rank of colonel. His assignments included duty with the U.S. Navy mission to Haiti (1960-62) and command of a battalion in Vietnam (1969-70). For five years he was business manager for the U.S. division of a major British international corporation. In 1982 he joined the Army Strategic Defense Command (DFC). After serving in the SENTRY Project office, he transferred to the PERSHING Project Office of the Army Missile Command, and subsequently became the deputy of that project. There he was deeply involved in the execution of the Intermediate Range Nuclear Forces Treaty with the Soviet Union. He served six years as director of Weapons Systems

Management Directorate, with twenty weapon systems including HAWK, AVENGER, and DRAGON.

Dr. Paro has a Master of Science degree in management (Dean's list) from the U.S. Naval Post Graduate School (1968). He was designated a Distinguished Graduate of the Industrial College of the Armed Forces (1972-73) and obtained his doctorate in business administration from Nova University in 1986. Dr. Paro is presently serving as director, Security Assistance Management Directorate, U.S. Army Aviation and Missile Command (ANCOM), and is also serving as chairman of NATO Army Land Group 5, with purview over Short Range Air Defense.

His family consists of his wife Virginia, two sons, Eugene and John, and two daughters, Kelly and Victoria. Gene is an avid classical pianist. He told me his father was the first Eagle Scout in Paducah. He is himself an Eagle Scout with Palms, as is his son John.

THE ERNEST LACKEY FAMILY

My memories of experiences associated with various members of this family cover the period from the 1930s through the 1950s. There were Mr. and Mrs. Ernest (Carrie) Lackey and their seven sons. Brian K, a grocer, married to Ada L.; Ezzell, in insurance and married to Lillian C.; Hecht S., president of Taylor Real Estate and in broadcasting, married to Rebecca,; Herndon, in newspapers, married to Jeanette; Pierce, in broadcasting, married to Willye Cummings, Eula, Montana and Ruby; W. Prewitt, in broadcasting, married to Ethelyn D.; Ernest, Jr., in broadcasting, married to Mollie Shelton and Bonnie Bessire.

The Lackey home was at 2103 Broadway. During the early years that I knew them, all the boys had Sunday dinner at the family home. Carrie Lackey was a member of the Christian Science Church, at that time located at 14th & Broadway, where my family were members from the time we moved to Paducah in 1923. The only other Lackey that attended there was Hecht, who was single back in the thirties and was the last son to leave the family home. Hecht usually brought his mother to church on Sundays and if he didn't bring her to Wednesday night services, one of the other sons did.

The church usually sponsored two lectures a year, hiring speakers from the Christian Board of Lectureship in Boston. Whenever other Science churches in their towns had lectures, one of the Lackey boys would provide their mother with a car and she would take a carload full of other members. Frequently I would be the designated driver. Most often, Pierce would furnish his big car and there would be room for six.

Among those that usually went were Mrs. Linn Boyd, my mother Edna White, Mrs. Emma Katterjohn, Miss Rosa Kolb, and Miss Mary Scott. During World War II, I dated Pierce's daughter, Mary Bayne, now Mrs. Dan Dahl of Imperial Beach, California. She was an ensign in the WAVES, stationed in Washington, D.C., and I was stationed in Philadelphia.

As far as I know, there are only two members of the Lackey family still living here, Charles P. Lackey, son of Prewitt and Ethelyn Lackey, and Jane Lackey Blaine, daughter of Pierce and Eula Rivers Lackey.

There were three Lackeys who became mayors: Ernest (the father)-Paducah,1928-1932; Pierce-Paducah, 1940-'44; and Ernest, Jr. (known as "Dutch")-Hopkinsville, 1945-'49, 1957-'61, 1961-'65

LIVING ON NORTH 25TH STREET

May 12, 2001

NOTE - this story is the result of a telephone call from a man who told me his grandmother was Dorothy Ann Coltharp. He was visiting Paducah from Muncie, Indiana, and wanted to know where he could get a copy of my book, "*I Remember Paducah When...*"

In August 1943, during my last week at the Air Force Officer Candidate School in Miami Beach, I was invited to dinner at the home of Mrs. Dorothy Ann Kissling and her husband John. He was a pharmacist's mate in the Navy and had been stationed there only four weeks earlier. They had learned of my whereabouts from a notice in the Paducah paper. That was the only time I saw her after her marriage.

After our conversation was completed, I thought that it was hard to realize that "little Dorothy Ann" would be old enough to be a grandmother. I still picture her as the eleven-year-old girl who played in the neighborhood with my younger sister Edna back in the early 1930s. I remember she gave Edna a picture of herself in her Girl Scout uniform. I saw her infrequently as a teenager, when she was a drum majorette at Tilghman High School, but when World War II came along, she moved away.

The Coltharps lived in the two-story brick house painted white with several columns facing south on the corner of 25th and Park Avenue. Today it is the residence of Bill Feiler, a high school classmate of mine and a golf partner for the past ten years. My family lived across the street at 706 North 25th from 1930 until the death of my father in May of 1933.

We had moved there from Harahan Boulevard, where there were many boys and girls our age with whom we became very good friends. During the short time we lived on 25th Street, we did not develop close friends, as we found there were very few our age. We continued to spend our leisure time with our Harahan friends. This meant long walks home in the late afternoons, since we did not have access to the family car until our father drove it home after work. We did become acquainted with nearby neighbors. The Hopwoods were directly across the street. Ed and Lucille Yopp and their growing family were next door. Eventually they had about seven children (I lost count after we moved). Several doors north of us lived Earl and Beulah Curtis and children, Imogene and James. We became good friends in later years. In the next block west were the Kings and their children, Kruger and Fain. Later Fain married Leon Gleaves, another good friend. There were no other young people near us. The area was a fairly new subdivision in the early stages of development. North 26th Street, one block west of us, had only two houses on it. Beyond 26th Street was vacant property up to Noble Park. North 28th then had not yet been cut through from Park Avenue to the Cairo Road.

C.F. BOYLES FAMILY
HARAHAN NEIGHBORS

We felt especially close to the Boyles family who lived on Harahan Boulevard, directly across the street from us in the late 1920s. Clyde was in my sister Ruth's 1929 Tilghman High School class. He worked one summer in one of my dad's grocery stores. His sister Beulah was a few years younger and later married Harold "Hoppie" Futrell, one of the "Harahan Hoboes," a name we neighborhood boys called ourselves. In those early years, neighbors were friendlier and you were very much aware of activities up and down the street. There was no air conditioning or television then and front porches were in daily use in the cool of the evening. When you would take a walk up and down the street, you could hear the popular radio programs being broadcast from house to house. At 6 p.m., a walk from Jefferson to Park Avenue could be made and you could hear "Amos and Andy" without missing any of it. We lost our frequent contact with the Boyles after we graduated and moved out to North 25th Street in the early 1930s.

Harahan Hoboes-From Left, Forrest Ladd, Hoppy Futrell, Harry White, John Wilson

FOOD BROKERS

In the 1920s there were a number of food brokers who maintained offices downtown. Each had their own line of food packers and canners. Most of the major name brand companies marketed their products through brokers - companies like Campbell's Soup, Heinz, Van Camp's, Dole, Del Monte and Quaker. Some brokers represented only one brand of products like Godchaux Sugar, or Maxwell House Coffee. Before he became a full line broker, I recall that C.F. Boyles represented Snowdrift. When he became a broker, his office and warehouse was at 329 South 2nd Street. After his son Clyde graduated from Duke University, he entered the family business and operated it for years after the death of his father. Clyde's sister Beulie Boyles Futrell was bookkeeper for years.

James E. English was an active food broker for many years. Records show he moved his office around to various locations down town. For a while he was located on North First Street. In the 40s, his office was on the 10th floor of the Citizens Bank Building. He and wife, Dorothy Wahl English, lived in the English Apartments at Jefferson and Fountain Avenue. His son, Jim English III, was an announcer for WPSD for years and was a low handicap golfer.

Fred C. Hassman was a food broker from the 1920s. His son, Bob Hassman, took over the family business and operated it until his death in the l980s. Bob and I were members of the 1931 Tilghman High School class. His sisters, Loddie and Siddie, were pretty, charming and popular. Loddie worked at the Citizens Bank for years and married Donald Schmidt. Siddie married Lindsey McMahon and moved to Louisville.

Another early food broker was the Johnston Brokerage Company, which bought and moved into the old Nashville, Chattanooga, and St. Louis freight building at 3rd and Washington streets. Mrs. Minnie Johnston operated the business for years after the death of her husband. Later, their two sons, Robert and Jack, took over the business and operated it until they retired and closed the business.

Bill Backus, originally from Louisville, moved to Paducah

Food Broker's Warehouse

Food Broker's Warehouse

and took over part of the NC and St L freight house and operated his brokerage business from there for years. For a few years in the 1950s, one of his salesmen was Bill Dowling from Georgia, who became my good friend and golf companion. He married June Faulkner, a lovely Paducah girl. They later moved to Florida.

WORKING AT DAD'S GROCERY

When our family first moved to Paducah, we lived in the Napoleon Apartments on the south side of Washington Street near the corner of 5th Street. Our landlord was a widow, a Mrs. Gardner who also owned the Kennett, an identical four-unit apartment building directly across the street, where she lived. There were two units on the first floor and two on the second, with stairs in the middle. Although there were six of us, we apparently were not too crowded, for in a few months, mother rented one of the bedrooms to a bachelor who worked somewhere downtown. Dad's first store, at 621 Broadway, was a little less than three blocks away, within easy walking distance. On the southeast corner of Sixth and Broadway was the fine old home of the Weil family, who later demolished the home and had the Irvin Cobb Hotel built there.

Dad had given up his job with the Broadway Coal and Ice Company in Memphis, a sales outlet for the West Kentucky Coal Company, to go into the grocery business. His store was the first to advertise as a "Cash & Carry" grocery. The biggest stores at the time were the Sloan Brothers at 12th and Jefferson streets, Bennett's grocery at 24th and Broadway and the Roof Brothers, over on the south side, at 7th and Tennessee. All ran charge accounts and made deliveries, so we were offering a new concept. The first store had a rail attached to all shelves that ran around the aisles at waist level, back to the front at the checkout counter. Near the entrance was a large bin filled with shopping baskets. To each basket handle was attached a hook with two small trolley wheels, so a customer could pick up a basket, set it on the trolley rail and slide it along the shelves while picking up cans, jars and other items as he or she moved around the store. When you got to the checkout counter, the rail ended and the basket would then be at a spot where the checker could remove the contents and add up the bill. When the basket was empty, the checker pulled down an overhead rope and placed the basket on a hinged overhead rail, then released the pull and the basket moved along the rail back to the bin. It was the forerunner of the pushcarts, which are now in almost universal use. After about a year, this method was abandoned, as customers would have to stay in line all around the store if they wanted to use the trolley baskets.

Another new wrinkle in the first store was a blower system designed to prevent flies from entering the store doors. An air compressor was installed in the back, which sent a blast of air through sheet metal ducts placed overhead and connected to ducts with narrow slits all around the door frames, so the air would prevent flies from entering when the doors were opened. Newspaper ads read,

"JUST THINK OF A STORE WITHOUT FLIES." Also near the front was a circular water fountain with about 12 jets of water and surrounded by a series of colored lights. The colors and the patterns of the spray changed every minute. Ads were placed which read, "DO YOUR GROCERY SHOPPING AT THE STORE WITH THE FOUNTAIN."

A few years later Piggly-Wiggly and other grocery chain stores were opened as the "Cash & Carry" concept caught on. In the early 1930s Dad opened his third grocery store at 16th and Harrison streets in a building constructed for him by Walter Mercer. The family had recently moved from a three-story frame house near the corner of Kentucky Avenue at 7th Street, to 316 Harahan Boulevard, across the street from Mr. Mercer who lived on the corner of Harahan and Madison. My father managed our number 1 store at 10th and Broadway, and my uncle Grady White ran store number 2 at 5th and Jefferson streets. Dad's cousin, Will Edd Barton, moved from Martin, Tennessee, to manage store number 3. Brother Harry and I were put to work at all stores weekends and after school, seldom together and sent where we were needed most. We both liked to work at number 3 best, as Will Edd was the youngest of the three managers and was more lenient than our dad and uncle. Also the flow of customers was not constantly heavy as at the other stores and the workload was much lighter. Will Edd was single, and nice-looking and a lot of the neighborhood women preferred to have him wait on them. I felt that some of them made more frequent trips than necessary and Will Edd was not one to ignore their interest. He had a southern accent and a very easygoing manner and many girls and women, most of them married, were attracted to him. I remember he carried on a mild flirtation with several of them, but to my knowledge, none ever got to a serious stage. Of course, I didn't know about his personal activities off the job and seldom saw him except at work. Usually there were only three of us working at one time. There was Will Edd, the butcher, and either Harry or me. The butcher and I took in all the "goings on" up front near the checkout counter and tried to guess Will Edd's favorite, and keep check of the most frequent customers and who would

Egbert Barton White

linger the longest. Our store was in the middle of a residential area, with most inhabitants employed by the Illinois Central Railroad Shops only a few blocks away. Dad made two visits daily, when he brought produce early in the morning and in the evening around six when he picked up the day's proceeds. Harry and I would have rather been out playing, but we made the best of it. We filled our time by loafing, playing around, and helping ourselves to apples, bananas, berries, cookies and nuts, at intervals all day long. We would occasionally snitch remnants of lunchmeats when the butcher was not around his shop area. He would wave his cleaver at us and threaten to do us bodily harm if he caught us trying to get into his meat case. We didn't know it at the time, and it probably would have stopped us if we had been told that he was working on salary, plus a commission on the profit his department made. So we were dipping into his pocket when we invaded his domain. But it was just a game to us and we never thought about the need to make a profit; we saw it as an opportunity to eat and enjoy all the goodies. Although we were paid the handsome salary of 25 cents a day for after school and $1 for Saturdays, the way we filled our stomachs all day probably made our net return ten times that amount.

Incidentally, when Dad opened his first grocery at 621 Broadway, it was named UNITED THRIFT STORE. Later after stores were added, they became the CLARENCE SAUNDERS STORES. During the last few years the name was changed to the WHITE FOOD STORES. The first name was franchised under a concern whose name was Hutchison Thrift Corporation. Dad learned after a few years that their stock was worthless and discontinued the association. Clarence Saunders was the founder of the Piggly-Wiggly chain and lost the business during the 1929 market crash, when creditors sold him out and took over the chain. Saunders, who also lost his palatial home in Memphis, (later opened as a museum and known as the Pink Palace) started a new grocery chain under the name, "Clarence Saunders, sole owner of my name." Dad teamed with Saunders then and continued until times started to get tough at the beginning of the Depression and decided to run his stores under the White name. The stores were always "Cash & Carry."

For a number of years the store owned no vehicles, as wholesalers delivered merchandise to the stores, and we made no deliveries. Dad walked to work, as our first three homes, which were rented, were not more that three blocks from store number 1. As branches were added, a truck was needed to operate between stores, so Dad bought an old second-hand model "T" Ford truck with no doors, a long bed and wire mesh side panels. After its purchase he began going down to the farmers' market at 4:30 in the morning for fresh vegetables. He would start out on one side of Kentucky Avenue near First Street and walk toward Second, buying what he wanted from a number of vendors who had their trucks or wagons backed up to the curb. Then he would go to the other side of the street for the few vendors that had come in late and couldn't find a space on the "good" side. From there he would go inside the Market House, where the growers with the bigger farms had leased stalls, which they kept for years. The center part of the building was reserved for the meat packinghouses. Next was an area for a few sellers of fancy fruits, and then on the west side towards Broadway were the farmers who grew and sold flowers. Stops would then be made at the several produce houses along Second between Kentucky Avenue and

Dad's Grocery, 621 Broadway, 1923-In Front, Barron and Harry; Dad, seventh from left; Uncle Grady, next left; Others, clerks and suppliers

Washington. The ones I remember were Barger & Golightly; H & H Produce, owned by Humphrey and Hopkins; and the Peck Brothers. Then Dad would load up and deliver to all stores. He got me up many a morning to go along and help. I first learned to drive on that old truck with the three floor pedals and a hand accelerator. I remember they kept that truck while Harry and I were in Tilghman High School. I recall this, as Harry had fallen out of the truck, which ran over his left ankle, crushing it. Dr. Warren Sights did a great job of setting it. Harry was on crutches for several months, and during that period we rode in the truck to school and I can remember getting out and getting him the crutches from the back end. When the Depression got real bad in 1933, many Illinois Central shop people lost their jobs and took their grocery business to stores with credit. Meanwhile Dad became sick and died and we lost the stores to creditors.

800 BLOCK, WASHINGTON STREET

After our family had been here a few years, we became familiar with which sections of Paducah were residential, and
where the commercial and industrial areas were located. We
knew that many of the blue-collar workers lived on the south side,
while most of the merchants lived on Kentucky or Jefferson; that the
majority of Illinois Central Railroad employees had homes clustered
within a few blocks of the I.C. shops on Kentucky Avenue, and that
many old-time Paducah families had fine homes in the West End.
Most African-American families lived either from 8th to 13th
between Washington and Caldwell, or from 9th to 14th from
Monroe to Burnett.

During my junior and senior high school days, I worked at
my father's grocery at 10th and Broadway. The store was "Cash &
Carry" and was not set up to make deliveries. We had only a single
1923 model "T" Ford ton-and-a-half truck that was used to pick up
from local wholesalers and growers.

Once when my assignment was to sack and carry groceries to
customers' cars, we had a request to deliver an unusually large order
to the customer's home. I heard the customer make the request to
my father and knew that he would tell her that we did not deliver.
So I was very much surprised when I heard him tell her that we
would make an exception and would arrange delivery later in the
day. The customer was not one who traded with us regularly and I
had no idea who she was. She was a nice refined-looking woman,
matronly, with pretty white hair and wearing expensive-looking
clothes.

While several clerks began to help load up our truck, I asked
my father for permission to make the delivery. I had been an alternate driver since I had turned 16 and had begun to make some of
the pickups from the Market House - and was eager to get as much
driving experience as possible. I thought Dad had not heard me,
since he made no answer, so I asked him again if he would let me
make the delivery. He gave me a stern look and a very emphatic,

"NO." He said that regular driver Glenn Campbell would take it. I thought nothing about until later after Glenn returned and told me he made the delivery to 813 Washington Street in the well-known "Red Light" district. Annie Redmon, the house madam, who had made the purchases, signed the check. That was my first up close look at one of "Ladies of the Evening."

SUMMER WORK

It was summertime in the early 1930s when for some reason that I don't recall, both Harry and I were working at Dad's number 3 store at 16th and Madison. It was unusual, since I was assigned to work Mondays through Fridays, except Tuesdays, which was when Harry worked. He had conned Dad into thinking I was more mature and more dependable, so he got to goof off most of the week. He used to moan and groan when his day to work came around and complained to both Dad and Mother each time. Harry loved to play tennis and played almost every day he could and became an excellent player and could beat me easily, much to my dismay and chagrin. I thought I was as talented, but used the excuse that I had to work all the time and didn't get the time and opportunity to develop my skill.

So, that time we were both working at the store. The storefront was all glass with another large plate glass window near the left front, looking out on Madison. The street was torn up, as the local gas company was tearing out all the old gas pipes and replacing them with new ones. It was around noon and we were not very busy. Two employees of the gas crew came in to buy something for lunch. Both went to the back and each got a bottle of milk. They then came up near the counter and each selected a small package of Hostess cakes. They paid their bill and went out and sat on the curb by the side window to eat. Soon one came back in and brought one of the empty milk bottles and said he was still hungry and wanted something else to finish with the rest of his milk. Harry pointed to some doughnuts in a glass case on the checkout counter. There were about a half dozen left from over the weekend and they were stale and hard. Harry asked, "How about two of those sinkers?" The man said, "Okay," so Harry sacked two in a small bag and the man again went out to finish his lunch. Soon the man was back, and as he returned his bottle he remarked, "Damn, those were the oldest doughnuts I ever tried to eat. When you called them 'sinkers,' you weren't kidding."

Dad bought an old 1923 four-door Dodge sedan for $100 from Morris Baskin, who owned Paducah Hide & Junk Company and used it to haul produce from the market. He took out the back seat and had a platform built to fit on the front bumper, so it would hold crates. We had no family car and when it was needed after store hours the front platform was removed and the back seat was taken out of our garage and put back in, so the family could ride. It was solid black and a good sturdy vehicle, as all Dodges were in those days. Dad and Mother seldom used it for personal runs around town (it was old and worn) but when Harry and I became old enough to drive, we took it out every night on dates. We literally ran the wheels off of it and put more miles on it in one night than it got at work in one week at the store. Sometimes stray pieces of food got caught under the seat and there was always some food odor. But it ran.

EARLY DAYS ON THE RIVER FRONT

When I first heard of Petter Supply Company, I didn't even know exactly where it was or what they sold. I knew the building faced the river on First Street and that was all. There was no floodwall then. I learned that the company was housed in an old two-story brick building that had been used as a hospital during the Civil War. The warehouse behind the main building extended all the way back to Maiden Alley. On the north side was a big lot used for storage and on the south side was "Bo" Anderson's blacksmith shop. Bo was the typical village blacksmith -

big, muscular and very intimidating to this greenhorn, when I had an occasion to make a delivery to him.

On the corner of First Street and Kentucky Avenue was Jackson's Foundry and Machine Company, run by "Pa" and "Ma" Jackson. Their son Charlie did all the foundry and welding work, while Ma kept the books. Pa presided over all. He wandered in and out at his pleasure, carried himself with a serene and contented look, and did not get involved with the daily hassle as Charlie did. He kept himself aloof and above it all. In contrast to Ma and Charlie, who always had dirt and grease on their work clothes, Pa was always neat and clean and cut quite a figure with his white tie, white moustache and beard and snow white hair. His pilot's cap was always at a jaunty angle.

Armour Packing Company had its plant on the river side of First and Broadway, with a rear unloading dock facing the river. The old Fowler Wharfboat was still there at the foot of Broadway, but was primarily used for storage. On the northwest corner of First and Broadway was the old Richmond House, used as a home for transients, then torn down after the 1937 flood.

A YOUNG MAN'S INTERESTS AND PURSUITS

A.B. CHALK AND SEAPLANES

In l940 and 1941, my brother Harry and I took a civilian pilot training course and acquired licenses to fly. We flew out of Howell Field on the Coleman Road, then Paducah's municipal airport. Our instructor was L.E. "Toogie" Galbraith, airport manager and owner of Galbraith's Flying Service. The course included instruction for 35 hours, with all flights being made in a model J3 Piper Cub. We began our training in October and received our certificates in March of 1941. The airport was less than a mile south of the Ohio River and we frequently flew over the river while practicing various maneuvers. The land near the river was flat and convenient, in case we might have to make an emergency landing, which we never did. We would occasionally sight other aircraft in the air in and around the airport, but this was no problem.

On more than one occasion we saw a twin-engine seaplane flying around the airport and once saw it land on the river upstream of the Irvin Cobb Bridge that connects Kentucky to Illinois. When we asked Toogie about it, we were told the plane was owned by the Chalk Flying Service of Miami, Florida, and flown by owner A.B. Chalk, a native of Brookport, Illinois. He said Chalk visited his homefolks several times a year. He had moved to Florida and built a good business ferrying Floridians to and from the islands in the Caribbean. Years later, when we took our young children to Florida we would see a Chalk seaplane pulled up on the bank of the causeway between Miami and Miami Beach. Although we intended to stop and meet him, we never did. By that time he owned several planes.

Last November I stopped in Kirchoff's Deli, across from the Market House Museum, and had coffee with the morning group of "boys," all longtime friends: Ralph Nagel, Bill Backus, J.C. Dudley, Sam Boaz, Pete Grimes, Sid Fulton, Rupert Stivers and others. Sam Boaz mentioned that his daughter in Charleston, West Virginia, had sent him an article in the Air Progress magazine about the Chalk Flying Service. He made me a copy, which included the complete history of the company. This is what I had been searching for.

In 1911, Arthur B. Chalk, age 22, was working as a mechanic in a garage in Paducah. Tony Janus happened to be flying on the riverfront in his Benoist single-engine flying boat, when he suddenly developed engine trouble. Chalk made the repairs and Janus gave him flying lessons in payment. Chalk acquired a Curtiss-Wright Jenny biplane and began to barnstorm around the southern and western United States. While flying in the Miami, Florida area, Chalk decided to stay. He traded his Jenny in on a flying boat and began operations from the docks of the Royal Palm Hotel at the end of Flagler Street. He established the Red Arrow Flying service and served Bimini in the Bahamas. Before long he added a Curtiss model F seaplane and expanded his service to Nassau.

When the United States entered World War I, Chalk joined the Marines and flew in the Air Corps. He returned to Miami after the war and resumed his flying service. He got his first real break in 1919. With Prohibition in effect, his passenger business all up and down the East Coast line zoomed. For centuries the proximity of the many islands to the mainland had been a smuggler's paradise, and although Chalk was not engaged in smuggling, many wealthy smugglers who brought their goods ashore by boat would use Chalk's air service to get back and forth. It was a convenient way to

Arrival of Santa Claus in his hydro-areoplane for Rudy's-December 13th

get to Miami to make arrangements.

In 1926, Chalk built a terminal in a newly created landfill, which became known as Watson Island on the MacArthur Causeway. He continued to enjoy good business, even after the repeal of Prohibition. He was said to carry many famous passengers to the Bahamas, including Howard Hughes and Ernest Hemingway. During World War II, Chalk donated his planes and services to the Civil Air Patrol and flew hundreds of anti-submarine patrols off the coast. After the war, Chalk upgraded his fleet with modern Grumman seaplanes. One of the first thousand licensed pilots in the United States, he continued to fly until 1966, having logged nearly 17,000 hours of flight time. He took pride in the fact that no passenger or pilot was ever killed in an accident during his years. In 1977, Chalk died in Miami and his company was sold. Since then it has had several owners, and as of the last report was still in operation in Florida.

So, Tony Janus, who taught A.B. Chalk to fly here in Paducah, can be given a lot of credit for the development and success of the seaplane industry in the United States.

HELICOPTERS
AND MOVABLE WING PLANES

Ever since the first time I flew in an airplane in the early 1930s, I have had an interest in flying. Other stories that I've written since were about learning to fly in a Piper Cub in 1940. And my three-year service in the U.S. Air Force was working close hand with four squadrons of Republic Thunderbolt P-47 fighter aircraft. Since then I have been fascinated with helicopters, but until this August, I had never flown in one. When Zelma and I went to the World's Fair in Seattle, Washington, in 1961, we noticed that a firm was renting helicopter rides from a pad atop one of the buildings. The aircraft was big and noisy and flew back and forth over the fairgrounds constantly during the daylight hours. It probably held six or more passengers at a time. There was always a long line waiting to take a ride, so we didn't want to stand in line and waste time, so we didn't go.

Then about twelve years ago when we were in California, we decided to drive down to Long Beach to see Howard Hughes' Spruce Goose, at that time the largest plane ever built. It was driven by eight engines and had room for 700 passengers. It was constructed entirely of wood and made only one flight for a distance of one mile at an altitude of 70 feet above the water. Hughes was at the controls. After touring the museum in which the plane was stored, we toured the *Queen Mary*, which was docked alongside the museum. Our Air Force 303rd Fighter Wing had crossed the Atlantic in the *Queen Mary* en route to the European theater during WWII, so a tour of this ship brought back many memories for me. When we left the ship tour, we noticed we could take a helicopter ride from a small field adjacent to the ship. I wanted to take my first ride, but for some reason I don't now recall, never did.

This March, the Paducah Chamber of Commerce held a trade show in the gymnasium of the Paducah Community College. While manning the booth containing over fifty of my pictures of old

Paducah buildings and scenes, I saw that visitors were invited to inspect three of Farrington Airpark's aircraft, parked just outside in the grass plot between buildings. These planes included two heli-copters and one heliplane. Benjamin Canady, flight instructor for Farrington, was on hand to explain the workings of each plane. He mentioned that flight training was available for all aircraft. I asked how much a demonstration flight would cost and was told $50.

When our community college seniors group began to select classes for our fall program, I suggested that we include a tour of Farrington's Airpark, for Instructor Canady had mentioned to me that although their operation was known all over the United States for manufacture and repair of movable wing aircraft, many people in Paducah didn't even know they existed. I felt this should be reme-died. After this was approved and included in our program, I made several trips to the Airpark on Shemwell Road, so I could make arrangements with Canady to set up a class and to learn what roads to take to get there. We agreed on September 9 at 10 a.m. to hold the class. On my last visit I mentioned that I would like to take a ride before the class, so I would be familiar with how the plane oper-ates. Canady told me he would not only take me for a ride, but would have me flying the craft before we landed.

First we went upstairs into a classroom, where an explana-tion of how all the controls operated was given. This was quite tech-nical, with a lot to be absorbed in a 15-minute talk. He explained that the helicopter's main rotor and tail rotor do the same job as the wings, propeller and rudder of an airplane. Lifting power of a rotor blade depends on the angle at which the blade meets the air. A "col-lective pitch stick" on the left side of your seat controls the main rotor blades to make the helicopter hover and fly straight up or down. To fly up, the pilot pulls the stick up; to fly downward, he pushes the stick down to decrease the pitch of the blades. To hover, he sets the blade at the medium pitch. On the handle is a throttle, which can be moved right to increase the power, sent to the rotor for upward flight or moved left to decrease the power for downward flight. The "cyclic pitch stick," set between the pilot's legs, controls the main rotor blades to make the helicopter fly forward, backward,

Don Farrington's Gyroplane on display at Paducah Community College.

or sideways. The pilot pushes the stick in the direction he wishes to fly. The "tail rotor pedals" control the pitch of the tail rotor blades to turn the helicopter right or left.

From there we went to the two-passenger Robinson R-22 helicopter parked on a pad near the hangar. We climbed into the side-by-side seats, donned helmets and earphones and turned on the radio so we could talk to each other. The dashboard was filled with a large number of dials and gauges, including air-speed indicator, tachometer for engine rpm, altimeter, horizon level dial, bank and turn indicator, and many other gauges, primarily for special planes used for training and not required for normal operation. After going through an explanation of the uses of each, we were ready to fly. The battery switch was turned on and the rotor blades began to turn. After a short interval, the blade pitch was changed and we lifted off to an altitude of 40 feet, where we hovered. We made a right turn with the right rudder and made a 360-degree circle, checking for other traffic to see if we were clear to continue. Then up and off we went on a flight at about 1000 feet over to 1-24 and near the river. Various maneuvers were made and explained as we made a big circle and headed back to the field. As we neared the field, we noted the direction of the windsock so we could make an approach up

Barron and Don Farrington, Farrington Air Park

wind. The instructor at that point cut off all power to demonstrate that we could make a safe landing even if a power failure were experienced. We glided gently down, with the blades continuing to rotate until we made a gentle touchdown in the grass strip along the runway. I had been on the controls all the way, with the instructor telling me what do and overriding my control if I failed to make the right moves. Then he took the helicopter up to about sixty feet, pointed it at the windsock and told me to fly in a straight line toward it. He took his hands off of the controls and said it was up to me. As soon as I took over, the plane began to turn right, which I tried to correct by giving left rudder. That did bring it back, but I also had pulled up the collective pitch stick causing the climb. I floundered around some for the next five minutes and know I did a sloppy job. I forgot everything he told me and reacted by instinct and did what I used to do when I flew Cubs. Then he took over and took us back to the landing pad. It was quite an experience and made me realize that a pilot on a helicopter has to be "on" the controls constantly with both hands and both feet flying the craft. I have more respect for those who fly movable wing aircraft and know it is not as simple as the standard fixed wing plane. I don't know if I'll try again, but if I do, I know what needs to be done and feel that I can do it.

BROADWAY
A CENTURY OF CHANGE

Broadway is the MAIN street in Paducah. It divides the North Side from the South Side, divides Upper Town from Lower Town, the former being up river and the latter, down river. By the middle 1920s, when we arrived, Broadway was primarily a residential street, with 83 percent of buildings being private dwellings.

Of a total of 224 buildings between 7th and 32nd streets, 186 were residences. Many prominent people of those days lived on Broadway. Brack Owen (whose family owned Owen's Island), H.D. Nichol (Paducah Lumber), Saunders Fowler (steamboats), George Langstaff (lumber), Louis Rieke (dry goods), H.J Livingston (wholesale grocer), Gus Thompson (horseman), Jack Major (entertainer), E.J. Paxton (newspaper), Linn Boyd (ice manufacturer), Frank Boyd (physician), W.F. Bradshaw (banker), Edgar Hamilton (mattress manufacturer), Wayne Seaton (mayor), Bill Dunbar (druggist), Joe Price (judge), L.S. Dubois (wholesale drugs), Frank Golightly (produce), Ernest Lackey (mayor), James Weille (men's clothing), J.A. Dossett (lumber), Robert Reeves (banker), Fred Lack (wholesale grocer), John Keiler (theaters), E.B. Willingham (physician).

Broadway had five churches: St. Frances deSales, Broadway Methodist, Temple Israel, Grace Episcopal, and First Church of

Junction of the Ohio and Tennessee Rivers at Paducah, Kentucky.

Christ, Scientist. Other buildings were: Washington School, Illinois Central Hospital, Carnegie Library, Fire Station #5, Paducah Railway car barn, Owen Bros. Dry Cleaners, Thompson Transfer, Williamson Granite, Marble and Stone, The Central Hotel (at the railroad tracks at 11th), five groceries, four drugstores, two restaurants, Dossett Lumber and several service stations. By 1950, Broadway contained 283 buildings, of which 188 were residences; the ratio then became 66 percent residential.

At year 2000, Broadway had 139 buildings, with only 14 residences - a drastic change during the century from 83 to 10 percent residential. There are no more than two residences from 19th Street east to the river, although there is an increase in the number of people living in the upstairs floors of their downtown business property.

OWEN'S ISLAND, VALENTINE OWEN, PADUCAH FERRY

Owen's Island lies on the river near the foot of Washington Street. It is over a mile long, widest on the upstream end and tapers to a point on the downstream end. It separates the Ohio from the Tennessee River about a quarter of a mile from Livingston Point and about 200 yards downstream of the Cuba Towhead, also called the Duck's Nest. Actually, the Ohio and Tennessee rivers first come together at Livingston Point, then divide at Owen's Island.

Among the early adventurers was Captain Valentine Owen (1803-1874), who at age 19, began his journey on the Ohio River at Louisville in a canoe and made the trip downstream alone. This was 1822, when a river journey was very dangerous. He was the grandson of Colonel Brackett Owen, who fought with William Henry Harrison when he was governor of the Indiana territory. He was a nephew of Abram Owen, who was killed in an Indian battle at Tippecanoe. According to his granddaughter, Ann Brackett Owen, he asked his friend Harrison to exchange horses with him, which Harrison did without a question. When the Indians saw the beautiful black horse, they assumed this was the leader of the militia and shot Colonel Owen.

When Valentine Owen moved from Shelbyville to Paducah, he learned that it was difficult to travel from Paducah to Illinois, so he started a ferry and it prospered. He began to operate a fleet of ferryboats that had a capacity of four horse-drawn wagons. His boat, "Bluebird," had a capacity of 72 tons. Stops were made at Golconda, Brookport and Smithland. For years, the ferry was the only outlet to southern Illinois.

Owen bought much land and leased other properties, which Indians worked for him. This included farmland in Kentucky, Illinois and the land facing Paducah, which was surrounded by water and known as Tennessee Island. General William Clark leased this island to Owen in a document dated May 9,1829. It read, "William

Clark leased to Valentine Owen a tract of land on the Ohio River below the mouth of Island Creek, for the term of one year. In consideration of the lease, Valentine Owen agreed to put up a good log cabin, corncrib, and stable and to enclose the cleared land with a good fence, and deliver possession of all premises to William Clark at the expiration of the lease. Signed, William Clark, Valentine Owen, Robert Fletcher."

Before he married in 1830, Owen built a frame house facing the river, between Kentucky Avenue and Washington Street. A few years later, he built a three-story tavern called the "Rising Sun," at the northeast corner of First and Kentucky, overlooking the river. According to his granddaughter, a teacher, who was interviewed some years ago when she lived at Superior Care Nursing Home, Owen's Island was a canebrake until long after the Civil War. As a child, she said she liked to go over there and picnic. She said that a group of men built a cabin on the Ohio River side near the head of the island. She recalled that her grandfather took whatever job he could find and after a while was able to buy bottom land in Illinois. When he died in 1874 he owned more that 2,000 acres of Illinois land.

Descendants of Captain Valentine Owen bought Owen's Island more than 100 years ago, according to early records. In 1894, his sons, James, Robert and Henry, were operating the fleet of boats owned by the Paducah Ferry Company. They were the "Bettie Owen, "Transport," "Market Boy," "The Ferry," and the "Owen." They made ten trips daily between Paducah and Brookport. Other business interests included the 3,000-acre farm on Owen's Island, managed by Robert Owen, and warehouses and a transfer business, managed by Henry Owen.

Later descendants include John Owen, a tall, good-looking young man a few years older than I. John lived at 710 Broadway in the 1920s when I first moved to Paducah. He was already out of school and worked at Gulf filling stations down town. I lost track of him in the late 1930s.

LIVINGSTON POINT

In earlier days Livingston Point had a sandy beach, but the intervening years have seen flowing waters wash it away. The point was a popular area for boaters to land, sunbathe, picnic, swim and camp, sometimes overnight. Many boys around my age would take dates there on weekends. We would launch our canoes at the foot of Broadway and paddle up the Tennessee River side of the island, spend a few hours at the point and paddle back. Some would swim alongside on the way back. Occasionally, some would return on the Ohio River side, which took a little longer, but was less crowded.

The Tennessee "chute" was always a busy area, with many boats and barges tied up to the island. There were three gasoline docks and unloading stations at the mouth of Island Creek, which flowed into the Tennessee just west of Elizabeth Street. Several Gulf or Standard Oil barges usually were docked for unloading. From there to Broadway there were a number of docks where fuel and supplies were available for business and pleasure craft. Towboats for Igert, West Kentucky Coal, Walker Boat Yard, Sangravl, Fred Olcott, and others plied the channel daily. So those in canoes and skiffs had to be constantly on the lookout for these bigger, heavier and faster

Canoeing on Tennessee at Livingston Point, June Faulkner and Barron

vessels. The activity lessened considerably in the late afternoon hours.

Among those with canoes were Ed Hank, W.L Beasley, Gene Katterjohn, Jimmie Yeltema, Taftman Abernathy, "Pug" Robertson, and many others.

ATHLETIC ENDEAVORS

TENNIS

From a very young age, I longed to become a good athlete. The very first time I had an opportunity to try any sport was when I was ten and lived next door to a tennis court. We had moved into an upstairs apartment at 8th and Kentucky Avenue and I could look out of my eastside bedroom window and watch tennis games all day long. The court was owned by a group of young men who worked downtown and used the court from 4 p.m. until dark. Neighborhood kids were allowed to play during the day until the owners showed up. We youngsters were required to take care of the clay surface and keep the chalk line markers in good condition. After a rain, the court lines required re-marking.

There were enough neighborhood boys to keep the play continuous. Some were my age, some a few younger, but most were a little older than my brother and me. Those who arrived first would flip a coin to see who could be first. The winner after three games continued to play until he lost or was tired and allowed another to take his place. We played singles most of the time, but if there were a large number waiting for their turns, we would play doubles. Owen Cummings and my brother Harry soon became the dominant players and got to play the most. I was always just an average player, usually better as a doubles partner.

During high school and for a while afterwards, a group of us played tennis regularly at various tennis courts at Barkley and Noble parks and at the courts of friends Tom and Mariann Clark, R.V.

Barron and
"Dub" at Barkley
Park

John Iler, Barron
White, "Dub"
Beasley and
Pershing Rogers
at Barkley Tennis
Court.

Owens and Joe Whitaker. Once I entered a city tournament on a court at 16th and Jefferson. I lost in the first round to Bill Berry, a former high school all-around athlete, who beat me, 6-1, 6-1. Some of the players I recall were Walter L. "Dub" Beasley, Joe Beasley, John Iler, Gene Funkhouser, Murl and "Speedy" Hogan, and Pershing Rogers. Harry played on the Tilghman tennis team and won most of his matches. Later I became interested in golf and quit playing tennis.

SOFTBALL

During the four years in high school our one-hour gym class included softball games inside on the basketball court. The grounds around the school did not include a ball diamond, only the football field with the track around it, so we had to play indoors. We had first base and home plate under the basketball goals. Several of us got to be good hitters and could pound the ball into the stage and score home runs. We hit the showers after thirty minutes, so we could be able to make the next class. After our class graduated, a number of us joined the popular softball league, which drew very large crowds to the ballpark just west of Noble Park. It's still there, but was enlarged to include several diamonds. We played for several years.

During the first half of the 1930 decade, softball at Noble Park was the most popular sport in Paducah, particularly in 1933 and 1934, when it reached its peak, drawing over 5,000 spectators every weekday night. Competition was intense among the 16 teams, which were divided into two eight-team leagues. It was a period when Harry and I were members of the Von Baron Ironclad Fraternity, a loose association of about 40 high school boys who played around town together. By the time we were all out of high school, we had rented a large three-story frame building at 23rd and Broadway across the street from the Ritz Hotel. The old building had been converted into a funeral home that folded after a few years and when we learned it was available, we jumped at the chance to rent it, as our old clubhouse was in a much smaller building. Members scrounged around for furniture and bought two pool tables and several ping pong tables for the lower floors. There were a number of boys who hung out there, and also at the corner drug store in the Ritz, across the street.

When the ball teams were being formed we got together to make up a team. All teams had sponsors, so we went looking for one. We were able to get the Dewey Payne Insurance Agency to sponsor us and provide us with uniforms and equipment. We were first named the Ritzy Ramblers, then the Dewey Payne Chryslers. As most other teams were composed of employees of the sponsoring firms, we were the youngest in age, since we were still teenagers. Our National League was composed of teams named Berghoff Beer, Paducah Sun-Democrat, Laundry Washouts, Volunteer Food, Goodyear Service, Paducah Cooperage, Lewis Frigidaire, and Worthy Manufacturing. Company. Our American League had Coca-Colas, Illinois Central, Farr-Better Supply, Dewey Payne Chryslers, West Kentucky Coal, Gilliam Candy, Paducah Box & Basket, and Kentucky Utilities. We were top contenders only one year, when we were beaten by the league-leading Cola-Colas in the title game, 15-11. Our team of youngsters was very often the crowd favorite and we were written up several times as the "big surprise of the current campaign." My regular position was left field, but I occasionally played third base. I usually was third in the batting order with my batting average somewhere in the middle of the pack. In 1935, the evening paper wrote, "POPULARITY TEAM AT MUNY TO PLAY FOR PADUCAH DRY." Rieke, Beaman, White, Gleaves and Mates to stay together again. The peppery band of youngsters known to Paducah softball fans as the Ritzy Ramblers and then the Dewey Payne Chryslers has found a sponsor. Paducah major league softball's youngest, liveliest club promised to a better-balanced team this season." Although we were not in contention for the title, we were not far from the top.

FOOTBALL

Some of the boys in my high school class became varsity football players. I applied for the job as team manager during my freshman year, but lost out to classmate Jimmy Distler, who happened to be football Coach Curtis Sanders' caddie-master at the municipal golf course in the summer. I was asked to work the scoreboard at all home games, which I did all four years. In my senior year, I decided to try out for football, although I knew I had waited too long to have any chance of making the team, but did play fullback on the scrub team. We provided scrimmage for the first and second teams during the weekly practice sessions after school hours. In addition, we played games against the junior high school teams that fed their best players into the high school program. One game in particular stands out in my memory. It was a game we played against Franklin (a former high school that later merged with Tilghman). Their star player was Marshall Jeffords, who later was a star player during his three high school years and was named to the all-state team. On one crucial play when our team had to kick to Franklin, Jeffords gathered in the punt on his 20-yard line and zipped through our line and backfield. I was the only man left between him and the goal line, so as he raced down the sideline I attempted to tackle him and knock him outside the line, but he threw a stiff arm to my jaw and sent me sprawling and continued until he crossed the goal line.

SWIMMING

The first time we went swimming, Dad took the family on the ferry over to the sandy beach right across the river from the foot of Broadway. A wooden change-house had been erected over the shallow water and wooden barriers were placed out at the limit of the shallow part with a sign warning swimmers not to go beyond the markers. Only Dad could swim, so the rest of us just paddled around. The small ten-passenger ferryboat made trips back and forth every hour all day long until dusk. We went over there once or twice for several years. This was in the 1920s and early 1930s.

During my first two years in the Boy Scouts in 1926 and 1927, summer camp was at Dixon Springs, Illinois, which is now a state park. At the entrance there was a general store whose owners took care of the swimming pool behind the store. This pool was fairly small, approximately fifty or sixty feet long and about thirty feet wide. Campers were permitted to use the pool one hour in the morning and an hour in the afternoon. Camp personnel supervised all periods with Boy Scout Executive Roy Manchester and several troop leaders as swimming instructors. Camp lasted two weeks and by the end of the second week, I could swim the width of the pool, confident that I could make it for longer distances without close supervision. By the second year, I felt I was a good swimmer.

Scout Camp Pakentuck near Ozark, Illinois, was in operation for my next two years at camp. In contrast to the Dixon pool, the new camp had a swimming hole formed by a small creek that had been dammed and was fed by a waterfall from a boulder seventy feet above the pool. There was no way to do laps in the circular pool and a large part of our time in the water was spent in diving from the springboard or from the ten-foot tower.

After the activation of the CCC camps in Kentucky, the Red Cross and CCC personnel sponsored a life-saving class at the Paducah Junior College pool at 708 Broadway. A number of us who swam at the pool regularly began working for our life-saving certificates, including Allard Hardy, John McNutt, Bob Dick Randolph, and Henry Kimble. After several weeks we all passed and were given badges to wear on our swimsuits.

Our swim coach at the YMCA/Paducah Junior College pool and the Noble Park pool in the summer was Paul Twitchell, a classmate who later became famous as the founder of a religion called "Eckankar." Paul assembled a swim team of boys including Burgess, Joe and Ed Scott, Gus Smith, Luke Nichol, George Barkley, Euclid Covington, Albert Otto, Allard Hardy, Clark Craig, Louis Fisher,

Paul Saunders, John Shelton, George Reeves, Artie Martin, Buster Sacra and me. My races were backstroke, breaststroke, and freestyle in the relays. George Barkley, Allard Hardy, and Albert Otto were the divers. All swimmers did not participate in every meet, but over the few years that we had a team, most did. We had competitive meets at home and away with teams of Metropolis, Cairo, Murphysboro, and Cape Girardeau. One meet was against a team at Memphis, Tennessee. We lost very few meets. I remember one time we lost a very close one against a small but strong team from Murphysboro. Our team also gave several swimming and diving exhibitions at the Noble Park pool, with large crowds in attendance.

One year Twitchell took a few of us over to Murray to give a diving exhibition to open up their pool for the season. I tried to become a diver, but could do only a few simple dives. So I became the clown diver, wore a loose oversize suit and performed several crazy contortions as I made my dives off the high tower springboard. Near the end of the morning show, the steps to the board were a little slick from divers walking from the pool to the base of the tower, so when I climbed to the top and took my steps to the end of the board, my feet slipped out from under me and I slid off the board, arms and legs thrashing and flailing as I hit the water with a big splash. The crowd loved it and gave me a big round of applause, not knowing that it was accidental and that it hurt as I landed on my back and side. I could barely crawl out of the pool, but stretched out in the grass to recuperate. As that was the last act, the crowd began to leave. For the next few hours I was in a lot of pain and had our trainer give me a rubdown and massage to my aching muscles. I was certain that I would not be able to perform at the evening show, but when the time came, I felt okay and did a repeat. Only this time I was careful to make sure that the steps and board surfaces were clear and dry. One small boy who had seen the morning show asked me if I would do a repeat of that last dive. I hated to disappoint him, but didn't do it, nor could I have. Harold Gilbert, a man now living in Paducah on Forest Circle just a short distance from my home, has reminded me several times in recent years that when he was a small boy living in Murray he was there and saw my "performance."

This is a swimming story that I almost forgot to include. This episode happened at the municipal swimming pool at Noble Park. I believe it was back in the 1960s, when the lifeguards decided to hold a swim marathon equal to the distance from Paducah to New Orleans, a distance of over 500 miles. This would be a continuous swim "round-the-clock" with each participant swimming a 30-minute time period. Since there were only half-dozen or so guards to fill the 48 time slots, each guard had to swim several times each day and night. After a few days of continuous time laps, local swimmers were invited to fill in. Although I had not been a regular swimmer for several decades, I had always been a good swimmer and wanted to participate, so I drove over one morning to sign up. The guard on duty, Sally Nemer, said she would see when a time was available. She said they were booked all that day but asked me if 4:30 the next morning would be suitable. I had assumed that surely they would have openings during the daylight hours, so told her that was too early. She then said she was signed up to swim the next half-hour and that I could take her place. That suited me, so I took it. I changed into my swimsuit in the clubhouse, and then jumped in when given the signal from the previous swimmer. I made a few laps back and forth across the width of the pool, when on the next lap back to the start, suddenly my arms felt full of lead; I could barely raise them to take another stroke. So I turned over to swim the backstroke that had been my specialty when I was on the team. During one stroke I took on a mouthful of water and was choking and floundering. Seeing my dilemma, Sally called out to me, "Are you O.K.?" I coughed out a "no." When I reached the side, she saw I was in no condition to continue, so she completed my period. I was completely exhausted and could not believe that I could've "pooped out" after such a short interval. I was embarrassed, but grateful that she bailed me out.

TRACK AND FIELD

B y my junior year in high school, I decided that I wanted to earn a Tilghman letter in athletics, given each year to members of the varsity football, basketball, and track and field teams. I determined that my best bet would be to get on the track team. I took journalism that year, our teacher being John Malcolm Longsdon, who was also track coach. Longsdon was a graduate of the University of Chicago and had been a member of their track team. He came to Tilghman in 1927 and found that the school did not have a track team, so he was given that assignment. Principal Walter C. Jetton had also come to Tilghman in 1927 and was a graduate of UK and the University of Chicago and had been a sprinter on an earlier Chicago team, so Longsdon was a natural choice. At our first practice, we were given wind sprints and endurance laps around the quarter-mile oval track that circled Keiler Field. Most of those who came out for track had been on the previous year's team, and since all milers had graduated, I was asked to run the mile. I was so eager to earn my letter that I agreed to try, but after two or three meets I found that the mile was not for me. At every practice session, milers were instructed to spend the entire time circling the track, to take a break every few rounds with a ten-minute rest, then one wind sprint. I decided I was not cut out to be a miler. So I asked to try the 220-yard low hurdles. I found that much more exciting and that I could win once in a while.

A funny thing happened one week when we went to Metropolis to compete at their track behind the school. While warming up, we discovered that the cinders spread on the track had come from the school boiler, and although most of the surface was fairly smooth, there were a number of lumps scattered around the oval. Since all races were run in lanes, a runner could not leave a lane without being disqualified, so you had to watch where you stepped. It was particularly hard on hurdlers, since you ran a rhythm, a certain number of strides between hurdles, always jumping off the same foot to clear the hurdle. Having to watch out for lumps made it

Tilghman 1931 High School 440 Relay Team-Left to Right, George Barkley, James Aarts, Barron White, Sam Gleaves

especially difficult. Jimmy Yeltema and I ran the low hurdles that day, with me in the first heat and Jimmy in the second. We ran a staggered start to adjust for the longer distance the outside man ran in his lane. Since I was in the inside lane, I used the starting blocks about ten yards behind my Metropolis opponent. When we reached the top of the first turn, I had caught up and was running side-by-side, and by the time I reached the backstretch, I was ahead by five yards. As I rounded the final turn, I was astonished to see my opponent ten yards ahead and about to cross the finish line. I knew he had not passed me but couldn't figure how he could be ahead of me. I learned that when the lanes were marked for a shorter race, they had marked a turn lane inside the long one that cut off about 30 yards. I had taken the longer one and the Metropolis man took the short one. We protested this, but lost. We made sure that Jimmy used the short lane and he did and won.

That summer at Boy Scout camp we had a track meet one afternoon and I found I could run the dashes. I was able to win every sprint race. So when I turned out for track my senior year, I won a place on the first team, running the 100 and 220-yard dashes and was number three man on the four-man 880 relay. George Barkley, a nephew of Senator Alben Barkley, was our fastest man, Sam Gleaves was second and I was third. Jimmie Arts was number four. We were strong in the track events with George Grimm, "Bang" Martin and George Morgan in the 440, Grimm and Morgan in the 880 and Jewel Booker in the mile. We had a good season, winning the Tilghman Invitational, the Murray Invitational, the West Kentucky Championships in Bowling Green, and an invitation to enter the 27th National Interscholastic Track & Field meet at the University of Chicago. Although we did not place in any of the individual events in Chicago, our 880 relay team won a sixth place medal, which we considered pretty good, since we were competing with athletes from 24 states. Now, 71 years later, I still have my medal from Chicago, in a small case hanging on the wall in my den. Incidentally, since our coach and principal were both University of Chicago alumni, they arranged for us to stay at their fraternity building overlooking the stadium. By the way, I did earn my "T" letter, which I wore on a Tilghman blue sweater.

BOXING AND WRESTLING

My only contact with this sport, other than as a spectator, was when I was in Washington Junior high School. This fine old building, which had been Paducah High School until Augusta Tilghman was constructed in 1921, was located in the middle of the block between 12th and 13th streets on the south side. It was made of yellow brick and was three stories high, with the gym on the third floor on the east end. Our gym teacher was Otis Dinning, who established a wonderful record as one of the most successful basketball coaches in the area, and who was later promoted to head basketball coach at Tilghman. He stayed at Tilghman until he retired and left a string of winning seasons that will be hard to beat. Otis taught us the fundamentals of all the major sports and a few minor ones, like boxing and wrestling. All students were encouraged to give every sport a try. In that way he could develop the ability of each boy where he showed evidence of special talent. Since Washington was training young boys just before their entry into high school, that time was a very critical period in their athletic development.

After a few encounters boxing classmates, I saw this was no game for me. I didn't enjoy hitting someone I could beat and derived no pleasure in being pounded by someone much better than I. Even today, I don't like boxing, think it is cruel, and should be banned. What pleasure can one get from seeing someone bloodied, with swollen features or being knocked out?

Wrestling, on the other hand, was quite different and fun. In contrast to today's professional wrestling, which is such a farce and merely an exhibition, amateur wrestling is not only a test of skill, strength and dexterity, it requires a lot of intelligence. On your first encounter, it takes a few minutes to size up your opponent, to learn his strengths and weaknesses, and how to plan your strategy. Of course, as boys in ages from barely teens to slightly older, we didn't learn all this in the two years that we were there.

During the sessions, each of us got to wrestle about six times with boys within our weight and size range. I recall wrestling Aris Rice (he won), Edson Hart (a draw), and Henry Wall (I won). There were several others, but their names do not come to mind. There were several clumsy boys whose physical prowess was late in developing, who were easy to pin despite being bigger and heavier. It was a matter of leverage and balance. Many matches were not completed, due to the time limit. It did not take long to learn one's limits. I felt I did fairly well and held my own most of the time.

BOWLING

The first bowling alley I remember was in the old Harbour Building on North Third Street, now occupied by the Carriage House Furniture Company. Sam Billings of

Billings Printing Company owned and ran it for a few years and many bowling leagues used their lanes for years. Some of us would go in for a few games now and then when lanes would be open, but most evenings were committed for use by the leagues. Brother Harry bowled with a group of fellow employees of the International Shoe Plant on North Second and Jefferson, but I was not interested then.

In the middle 1950s, after I became a member of the Paducah Rotary Club, a few members decided we should have a team, so I joined and became one of the regular players, along with Paul Pearce, Don Boucher, Carl Marquess and Merle Jones. We were in one of several leagues and bowled on Tuesday nights. We were competing with over a dozen other teams, bowling with a different team each week. I don't remember where we stood at the end of the four or more seasons I was a member, but we were never close to the top, nor were we ever on the bottom. Several team members were able to maintain a high average of around 200, but our team average was much lower. Several teams carried an average near the 200 mark and were consistently tournament winners. My average never topped 165 and was usually close to 160. One season our team flew to Bowling Green, Kentucky, to bowl against several Rotary teams in that area and came home with the trophy. I was out of town that weekend, and was not able to be a part of it. In the late 60s and early 70s, we used the alleys at Cardinal Point. When the Cabana Club was built on the south beltline, we moved there and stayed until the club was destroyed by fire. There came a time when I had to quit. I had developed swelling of the joints in both hands and could no longer hold or control the ball. Then, too, I found that my night-time activities away from home were getting to be a problem and decided to cut back to fewer nights away during the week. With two growing girls not yet teenagers, I needed to be home.

GOLF

I first knew there was a game called golf in 1920 when I lived in Memphis, Tennessee. When I was six, we moved from midtown to a suburban area called Buntyn, the last stop on the streetcar before the Memphis State Normal stop. Dad bought a five-acre lot and built on the back end facing the streetcar line. There was a large wooded area between our house and the Buntyn station. The Memphis Country Club was on the other side of the track and the eighth green and ninth tee were directly opposite our house, which you could not see, as the track was elevated about eight feet. We were told not to cross the tracks, but we could walk through a big concrete culvert under the track near the station. We would do this and stand at the barbed wire fence surrounding the course and watch members putt and drive. In those days, the men wore knickers and ties and we were told that golf was a rich man's game. On some days when there was no one playing, we would slip under the fence and play in the sand traps. They also had a sandbox they used for making tees. That was before the days of wooden or plastic tees.

After our move to Paducah in 1923, the municipal golf course was in Baumer Field, just west of Noble Park. When we moved to North 25th Street, we rode our bicycles there. The golf pro was Curtis Sanders, Tilghman football coach, who warned us not to ride on the course, as some bikers had been doing and making tracks through the sand greens. Jimmy Distler, a classmate, was caddymaster and when play was light, he would lend us a club and let us try to hit a few balls in the practice area. I thought it would be easy, since I could hit a moving softball, I should be able to hit a ball not moving. But it was just not that simple. After I was out of high school and working, I decided to try golf, since many of my friends were playing. I began to play at the municipal course, then at Lakeview, now known as Rolling Hills. Back then, it was only nine holes. I didn't have a regular foursome at first, but would just go out and pick up a game. After a short time, Kelly Crayne, a golfer a dozen years my senior, asked me to join his group, which I did.

While I was in the Jaycees, with encouragement and financial backing by Edwin J. Paxton, editor of the *Sun-Democrat* and its sports editor, Sam Livingston, the members helped raise the money to buy land to build an 18-hole course at the intersection of Jackson Street and the Lone Oak Road. The course was opened in the summer of 1940, with Mr. Paxton driving out the first ball. Mayor Pierce Lackey christened the small clubhouse and pro shop "El Bucko," in honor of Buck Burnett, the Jaycee who raised the most money. Brooks Starr became the first pro and played in the first foursome with Marion Miley, a popular woman professional golfer from Lexington, brought here for the occasion.

When the Edwin J. Paxton Municipal Golf Course opened, all former muny players moved to it. Kelly and I continued to play together. Our foursome changed over the years as some died, moved away or joined other courses. Until golf carts began to be used, everyone hired caddies, a number of whom were always on hand at the caddie shack, waiting to be selected. There were a number of good caddies who were always booked up and sought after. Many of them "grew up" on the golf course and became good golfers. I remember the Mullens and Bill Bone, Bill and Bob Berkley, and a few other caddies golfed at Paxton for many years. Daniel "Kayo" Mullen recently retired as pro at Paxton and at present his son Danny is the pro. Carts were prohibited at Paxton at first, until Ray Jacobs, a member of the golf commission, was permitted to use his there. Kelly Crayne was one of the first to buy a cart and it was several years before he was permitted to use his own cart, and then he had to pay a trail fee, as it is called. Now, the pro owns and rents all the carts at Paxton and that is one of his perks.

When I returned to Paducah in 1945, after three years in the service, I began to play more often. I became a member of the Paxton Park Players Advisory Board and served as treasurer several years. I played on the Paxton course team that had weekend games with and in other cities- Princeton, Madisonville, Mayfield and Fulton. My best game ever was at the Princeton Country Club, when I bested my opponent and shot a 78, a figure way below my rounds now. I had my only hole-in-one at Paxton about 30 years ago, a 5-iron shot on the 165-yard 14th hole.

Kelly, who owned an auto repair garage, was twelve years older and had been a very good golfer. As a beginner, it took me several years to reach his game level. Then in his declining years, I became the better player. But we always got along well together and enjoyed each other's companionship and the fellowship we had with other members of our foursomes. Among our last regular foursomes were Lee "Jelly" Hewitt and Randle "Flo" Floro. Others were Dr. Gene McGarvey, Dr. John Bryan and "Buster" Blackston. For several years I was active in the Associated General Contractors organization, our Petter Supply Company being an associate member. Every summer I would play in their golf tournament as a member of a foursome made up of several Petter customers. We always enjoyed the outing and occasionally won money or prizes. In 1972 I was the winner of the second flight individual low score.

Since 1982, my former employer, the Petter Supply Company, has held a golf tournament, open to employees, owners, factory representatives and a very few personal company friends. All matches have been held at the Kentucky Dam State Park at Gilbertsville, Kentucky. There are usually about 24 teams of four players, some with women. There are a few teams with five players. The park has always reserved the course for us on a Saturday morning in August, and as a shotgun start is used, with half the group off from number 1 and the other half off from number 10, all matches are over by 2 p.m. There is always an intense rivalry among the teams and always a large assemblage of players around the 18th hole to see how the teams scored. Then all participants drive the several miles on Sledd Creek over to the Petter cabins on Kentucky Lake, where a picnic awaits them. After filling up on barbecued pork and chicken, and washed down with soft drinks or beer, everyone gathers on the cabin patio to hear the final results and the handing out of prize money and merchandise. Prizes are given for first to last place, with prizes for longest drives, men; longest drives, women; and closest to the pin on the four 3-par holes. Also prizes are awarded for "skins," (the team that has the lowest score on each hole.) First prize is usually $500, with the last prize $20. The teams split the money. I have

Members of the Paxton Park Players Association-1950-Right to Left, Paul Sargent, (president), Tom Whittemore, Barron White, Bill Dowling, James Stephens-Photo taken during a planning session for the July 1950 Irvin Cobb Championship Tournament.

played in all but three, missing one while in the hospital and two while on vacation. Our team of John Ellis, Ron Overton, Frank Harwood and I, won first prize in 1984, shooting six under. This year, the 10th since my retirement, I am invited to play and plan to do so, barring unforeseen circumstances.

For several years four of us, all members of the local Rotary Club, would go south in the late winter for a weekend of golf. Louis Graybeal, former manager of the Western Kentucky Gas Company; Charles "Chuck" Heyduck, with Blue Cross-Blue Shield; Henry Mueller, a former pharmaceutical salesman; and I would go to courses down south around the Gulf for as much golf as we could crowd in for a few days. Chuck usually selected the spots. We've played at Biloxi and Gulfport, Mississippi; Fort Walton Beach and Destin, Florida; and Callaway Gardens and Stone Mountain, Georgia. We would spend a day, usually a Friday, at the PGA golf tournament at Memphis, Tennessee, watching the best pros on the tour.

When I retired in 1989, several friends persuaded me to join the Rolling Hills Country Club, where they were members. This is a beautiful course, very hilly as the name implies, and quite a challenge for an average golfer like me. I enjoyed playing there, but discovered that there were a number of foursomes that had been established before I joined and usually I got to play with close friends only when they needed a fourth to fill in for an absent member. And all of them had their own carts, which I didn't. So I decided to return to Paxton, where I could walk and pull a handcart, which is what I am doing at the present. My present companion is Bill Feiler, a retired pharmacist. George Grimm, a retired savings and loan manager recently passed away. Both were in high school when I was. We usually play just nine holes, which continues to be fun before getting tired.

BUD MOSS BARBECUE-1930

James H. (Bud) Moss was reputed to have the best barbecue locally, in a region which boasted the "best barbecue in the world." For years his tiny shack on the southwest corner of 10th and Caldwell was so well known that people came from all over. He was open only from 10:30 a.m. to 2:30 p.m. and resisted all pleas to expand or stay open longer. His small lunchroom was always spotlessly clean. He never touched the meat or bread with his bare hands; he would always slice the meat, then spear the bread with a long two-pronged fork, then serve open face on a plate, so the customer could apply the desired amount of Bud's special sauce to make their sandwich. His place was always so crowded at noontime that customers were accustomed to a short wait. As Bud had no helper and personally waited on all who came, he had everyone take a number as they came in, and then he would call out the numbers in turn, as they came and he prepared the order.

One day I decided to take a visitor to his place. We got there just a few minutes after it opened. We were his first customers of the day. Bud was busy behind the counter, trimming a pork shoulder. He looked up as we opened the screen door and walked inside. I spoke up and asked him to fix us two sandwiches. He asked, "What is your number?" As we were the only ones in the place, I gave him a quizzical look. Seeing my hesitation, he said, "Get a number there on the hook." So I reached up and got numbers 1 and 2, handed them to him and he proceeded to make up our sandwiches. After his death in May 1956, his widow Myrtle continued to operate the business for a few years. In 1965 the city built Blackburn Courts and took over several blocks, including the old barbecue site.

HEINIE AND TYLER

Many long-time Paducahans will remember this popular place that was on the west side of North Fourth Street between Broadway and Jefferson. Henry Steinhauer and Tyler White were Heinie & Tyler. They began in 1916 in the old Standard Newspaper four-story building at 115 North Fourth, and then in 1917 they bought the building at 119 North Fourth, that for many years had been the S.B. Gott Saloon. During their first years, they served alcoholic beverages, then when the Volstead Act was passed in 1919 and became the law of the land, they had to limit their liquid refreshments to "near beer" and soft drinks. To supplement their income they also added eight pool tables.

When Prohibition was repealed in 1933, they were again able to offer beer and liquor. They moved four of the pool tables next door to 117 North Fourth and put veteran associates, "Tosco" Rudolph and "Swede" Ruark, in charge. They offered sandwiches and pie, and probably served all downtown workers at one time or another. There were three tables, but most patrons stood up at the bar. Although no women were allowed inside, they could order "take-out" food from a window at one side of the front door. Their wieners and hamburgers became favorite noontime choices, in my view, because of the very special mustard they made fresh every day. Pickled pig's feet and boiled eggs were also popular items, kept in large glass jars on the bar. In the winter during the holiday seasons, a large bowl of eggnog occupied a prominent place on the counter behind the bar. The two sidewalls had full-length mirrors from front to back. On the east wall was a circular clock with figures in reverse and with counter-clockwise moving hands, so customers could tell the time through the mirror behind the bar.

The owners' sons, Adrian White and James Steinhauer, were associated with the business for many years. After Tyler White died in 1964, they continued to operate until July 1969, when they closed the business. So what had been one of the most popular food and drink places downtown for over half a century, became history with only fond memories of earlier times.

BOSWELL RESTAURANT

The Boswell Restaurant, which had been a fixture in Paducah for almost fifty years, came to an end in February 1957. Paducah Sun-Democrat reporter Bill Powell wrote a nice article noting its passing. He related how Ben Boswell cooked soup in a lard can for a hungry crowd in the office of his father's Mayfield wagon yard at the age of eleven. Farmers who had gathered there to swap knives and stories had gotten hungry. The soup, hot and thick, sold for a nickel a bowl and made C.W. Boswell's yard a very popular place. This experience led Ben Boswell into the restaurant business in downtown Paducah until he retired.

Ben was born on his father's farm in the Pottsville section of Graves County in 1899. He worked in the corn and tobacco fields there until he was 17. In 1906 he was a cook's helper at an independent wheat thresher, peeling potatoes and picking beans and turnip greens for the boss-cook as they moved around the county. When the cook got sick and left, young Ben took over the cooking. He recalled that for breakfast the men devoured heaps of bacon, rice, grease gravy, sorghum molasses and biscuits on tin plates handed down to them from inside the cook wagon. For other meals Ben cooked all the vegetables and meat they could eat. A few years later he took a job as a cook for Housman and Jeffrey's road building crew working across Graves County building roads that ended the dirt road period.

In 1909, Ben married Bertie Nance of Pottsville, a girl he had known all of his life. They farmed for a year with her helping with the work in the restaurant, in addition to the farm work. It was a cold wintry day in January 1911 when they moved to Paducah and rented a house at 4th and Monroe. He applied for a job as a street-car motorman, but the foreman said he was too small. Ben was five feet, four inches and weighed less than one hundred pounds. He remembered that farmers like to eat, and would pay for good food, so in February of 1911 he opened a restaurant at 202 Kentucky Avenue, in the building known today as Finkel's. As always, the Boswells worked hard to make the business a success. They sold ham and eggs for 15 cents, coffee and a doughnut for a nickel, rich stew for 15 cents and a porterhouse steak for a quarter. At the end of the first day they had taken in $8.75. They made money at the place because farmers liked the food and the courteous way they were treated. Two years later, Ben bought a saloon at 111 South Second Street. Mrs. Boswell became a housewife, as the law prohibited working women. He offered beer and whiskey "dirt cheap" and gave away free lunches to attract customers. A 12-ounce beer and a wiener, oyster, or boiled egg was a nickel; a half pint of whiskey was a quarter; a quart cost 75 cents.

Finding that he was not making money, Ben became a hired hand for John Clendenon at 113 South 2nd Street and worked in his saloon/food business for three years. He saw that the business was profitable and returned to the saloon business in the 100 block on South Second. Since free lunches were then outlawed, Boswell did well. His biggest day was June 30, 1918, the day before Paducah and the rest of the country went dry. So when liquor was phased out, Boswell entered a new field. He returned to Mayfield and went in business with others, and opened a car agency to sell Gardner and

Republic trucks. They had a disastrous year and he lost all that he had made. He returned to Paducah where he had started, in part of the building at 202 Kentucky, catering to farmers. Four years later, he moved to Broadway next to Lang's Drug Store, changed his style and directed his restaurant business to a mixture of farmers and business people, serving more expensive food and catering more to the after-dinner crowd.

The restaurant business did well until the Depression wave of 1929. They hung on for a while, but soon saw that they were going broke. But, in 1932, undaunted, Boswell walked up the street and with extraordinary courage rented the big Palmer House dining room from the Keiler estate with borrowed money. He began business in the dining room from the front part back to where the second level was. Later they took over the Palmer private dining room behind, doubling the size.

Soon the Boswell Restaurant became the favorite downtown eating place. Then the 1937 flood became another setback, as the waters surged through the restaurant and all over town. But before long Ben and Bertie Boswell were back in business. In 1944 they suffered a bitter double blow: their daughter Frances died unexpectedly after a short illness. Then, less than two months later, their 25-year-old son Charles died in a train wreck near Jellico, Tennessee, while en route to the Army.

Their other two sons, Ben Jr., born in 1912, and Morris, born in 1923, had become active in the business and enabled the parents to spend more time at their 17-acre farm and home on Highway 60 west of Paducah. When their lease of the dining room in the Palmer House expired at midnight February 15,1957, the Boswells decided to close the downtown business. Boswell said he was not forced to quit, but that it was a practical matter; what with paying rent, the high cost of keeping up the large dining room and the wages of the big crew, he could no longer continue to give the kind of service he believed in and continue to make ends meet. Anyway, he said, his sons, who were partners in the business, had since opened up a new Boswell's Park Avenue and they could give that venture their full-time attention.

A short time later in the 1960s, the 5th and Broadway corner underwent a drastic change. The Kentucky Theater, the Palmer House and several buildings east of the Palmer were demolished to make way for the J.C. Penney store and other businesses. So ended an era with fond memories of downtown Paducah.

BATTLE FOR THE NORMAL SCHOOL

In the early 1920s, Paducah was one of nine western Kentucky cities considered for the location of a state normal school. If Paducah had obtained the college, all those now living in the Avondale area would be living somewhere else. And those who went to Murray could have gone here to Paducah State University.

In the 1998 annual report issue of the Murray State magazine, the front cover read, "MSU FOUNDER HONORED". It featured the unveiling of the Rainey T. Wells bronze stature on the campus. The lead article stated, "Dr. Wells led the charge for Murray to accomplish what several towns in western Kentucky wanted to do. It was in 1922-23 that he proved himself a dominant force in influencing the general assembly not only to create the state normal school commission, but to pass legislation establishing two additional normal schools, one at Murray and one at Morehead."

In March 1922, then Kentucky Governor Edwin P. Morrow signed legislation to establish two normal schools in the commonwealth, one in the east and one in the west. How Murray became the successful city is quite a story.

The state legislature appointed a commission to locate the sites for the proposed normal schools. House Speaker James H. Thompson selected Judge E.C. O'Rear of Frankfort as chairman, and appointed W.S. Wallen of Prestonburg, secretary. Others appointed to the commission by Thompson were Sherman Goodpaster, Frankfort; T.A. Combs, Lexington; and E.W. Senff, Richmond. Lieutenant Governor L. Thurston Ballard appointed Alex Barrett, Louisville; J.L Harmon, Bowling Green; and Arthur

Peter of Louisville. Each competing city had raised $100,000 for the purchase of grounds and buildings, and had filled out a questionnaire setting forth the city's qualifications. The nine cities that competed for the western school were Mayfield, Owensboro, Henderson, Paducah, Murray, Benton, Clinton, Princeton and Morganfield. Representatives from each city were invited to appear at a hearing held on May 30, 1922 at the Seelbach Hotel in Louisville. The fifteen-member Paducah delegation consisted of J. Henry Rudy, chairman, and *Mrs. Edmond (Josephine Fowler) Post,* Mrs. Robert B. Phillips, Mrs. C.E. Purcell, Mrs. S. Elizabeth Tandy, *Miss Anne Baker, W.F. Bradshaw, James F. Smith, *James C. Utterback, *Charles Vahlkamp, *Richard Rudy, *Edwin J. Paxton and Frank Burns. (* I knew these personally.)

One of the sites offered by the Paducah delegation was Wallace Park, with its seventy-five acres of land, twenty-five of it woodlands. It was located on the streetcar line, had "splendid" roads leading to it and was within walking distance of the city proper. They also cited the abundance of daily train service, a network of fine roadways, good water, good hospitals, a fine library, and a "wonderful supply of fresh milk, and superior meat and vegetable sources." The hearings took two days, with Paducah, Benton and Murray held over until the second day. Clinton and Mayfield agreed that if their cities could not get the school, it ought to be placed in some other city west of the Tennessee River. "The (Jackson) Purchase is for the Purchase," they jointly stated.

On June 10, the Paducah delegation learned that the department of education would insist that the successful city be able to provide a building immediately, so the first class could begin the following September. The delegation dispatched a telegram at once to the commission offering the facilities of Augusta Tilghman, citing it as the "newest and most modern equipped in the state." (Tilghman was built in 1921). This offer would be temporary, until permanent facilities could be constructed. Later, State Superintendent Of Public Instruction, George Colvin, said the decision would not be made on the basis of a temporary expediency, but for the long haul.

On June 17, the commission announced it would tour all

the proposed sites, beginning with the western Kentucky cities, then to the eastern sites the following week. No selection would be made until all sites had been inspected. Each city would pay $100 toward the expense of the tour, which would begin July 17 in Owensboro. The commission was to arrive in Paducah by train at 4:10 p.m. Wednesday the 19th. Chairman Rudy announced that very elaborate plans had been made for the visit of the commission members. They would be escorted by car to their hotel, taken that evening for dinner and a dance at the country club, and be entertained at breakfast at the Palmer Hotel. Thursday morning they would inspect the proposed site, the I.C. Hospital, Tilghman High School, Carnegie Library and Riverside Hospital. Commissioners would be guests at a luncheon of the Exchange Club, and then leave for other west Kentucky towns. All week long the Paducah newspapers were filled with articles by prominent citizens and ads by local business firms, telling why Paducah was the logical choice for the school. The July 20 edition of the *Paducah Evening Sun* reported, "Members of the commission expressed themselves as being highly pleased with the site and facilities, which Paducah offers the normal school...and it was unanimously declared by the commission as being most satisfactory. If it is decided that the school be located in Paducah, the site offered is entirely satisfactory, according to a statement of Judge Edward O'Rear, chairman of the commission."

The commission went on to Benton, where members were guests of honor at a barbeque dinner on the grounds of the county courthouse, and then toured the site selected by Benton. Members of the Benton committee were A.A Nelson, Grover Treece, Joe Ely and Judge Joe L Price. I. R. Jones of Murray, a member of the state tax commission, accompanied the commission to Murray. A mass meeting of the Murray delegation greeted the commissioners upon their arrival at the Calloway County Courthouse. After talks the group toured the proposed site.

It was not until September 2 that a decision was announced. The headlines in the *Paducah News-Democrat* read, "MURRAY WINS NORMAL; VOTE IS WITHHELD." A sub-heading read, "Mayfield is Only Competitor as Paducah is Barred as Too Large."

The news of Murray's victory beat Wells home. Frenzied band music and a cheering crowd greeted him. He had pulled it off. After the meeting a member of the commission said that Paducah and Henderson, which had been regarded as contenders, were dropped out of the balloting after the first few votes, saying, "It seemed that the commission was opposed to the large town idea in placing the new school." The one-inch high headline of the September 4 *Paducah Evening-Sun* read, "NORMAL AWARD AROUSES IRE - O' REAR DEFENDS!" It reported that Mayfield was leading a battle to probe the award to Murray and that an investigation would be made of circumstances surrounding the choice of Murray by the commission. It was rumored that Murray was "slated" from the first. Judge O'Rear said, "I invite investigation, I challenge it and I defy it." He explained that the committee chose Murray because, "it made a showing that placed it ahead of other cities." Answering charges made by Homer W. Nichols of the Caldwell County schools that eastern Kentucky coal interests had "fixed" the selection of Murray in return for indulgence from the state tax commission, of which Rainey T. Wells of Murray was the chairman, Judge O'Rear said that the only representations that had been made by any coal company interests were in favor of Paintsville (for the eastern school site). Judge O' Rear said he voted for Henderson first, but the other commissioners voted him down. When Henderson was dropped, he said he voted for Clinton. Then when Clinton was dropped, he said he voted for Mayfield. When it appeared that there would be a hopeless deadlock, he then changed to Murray. "I even voted for Paducah once. I believe that such a school as this should dominate the community in which it is located, and not the community dominate the school, as would be the case with either Paducah or Owensboro," he said.

The Mayfield forces stressed claims that one of the wealthiest bankers of Murray sent a large sum of money to Mayfield early on, to be wagered on Murray getting the school at odds of 6 to 5 against the field, and the statement of a Paducah minister that one of the commissioners told him soon after the commission was appointed, that it was "fixed." The reported voting was that commission members selected by James H. Thompson - Chairman O'Rear, Goodpaster, former Senator Combs, County Judge Senff and Representative Wallen - voted for Murray. The three commissioners appointed by Lt. Governor Ballard voted for Mayfield. This resulted in five votes for Murray, three for Mayfield. An editorial in the September 6 edition of the *Paducah Evening Sun* leaves many unanswered questions that so far as I know, were never disclosed or answered. One statement reads, "Those who resent the charges that the choice of Murray was in accordance with a plan arranged before the appointment of the commission, must acknowledge that there would be less in appearance to suggest criticism, if all the votes received by Murray had not been made by those commissioners named by the speaker of the house of representatives."

For many of my earlier years in Paducah, it was rumored that a number of influential people in Paducah silently and secretly worked behind the scenes to prevent Paducah from getting the school. In all the research I made of old newspaper reports of this whole situation, I uncovered no proof that any Paducahan actually was against Paducah. Even those who suspected people at the Paducah newspapers were responsible, must be wrong, for owners and editors of the two big local papers were members of the delegation that worked to bring it here. I've heard that, "Politics are the damnedest in Kentucky," so who knows what actually took place. There may some few people still living who know the truth, but that would have to be "THE REST OF THE STORY."

BOSSIE FAMOUS - BOSS NOT

Jimmie Huston, for long years the subject of a Paducah mystery, was a lifelong friend. We were born the same year. We attended Boy Scout camp at Dixon Springs and Ozark, Illinois, for several years. He stayed active in the Scouts and served as troop leader at both Fountain Avenue Methodist and Westminster Presbyterian churches. He was a 1935 graduate of Augusta

Tilghman High School, where he played in the band. He was a member of the Rizpah Temple in Madisonville and the Rizpah Oriental Band, serving as vice president and director for 17 years. He was a Kentucky Colonel and a Duke of Paducah.

As we stayed in Paducah and worked here all our adult years, we saw each other regularly at restaurants, ball games and at many other events and activities. He retired from the Kentucky Highway Department for health reasons at the age of 85, on February 29, 2000. He died three months later. It was not until after his death that I learned he was the mystery man in one of Paducah's most whimsical mysteries.

Jimmie's daughter, Jimmelyn Huston West, now married and living in Benton, Kentucky, bought my first book last year and wrote to me, "I prepared this written account...from conversations with my father, during his last days. I asked him to tell me about when he put the cow on the balcony during the 1937 flood. When the artist (Robert Dafford) was painting the murals on the floodwall, my father went up to him and told him that he was the one. Dafford was astonished, said he had wondered, and those he asked didn't seem to know. My father was a very humble, unassuming man. He had a great sense of humor and held on to it even to his final days. My father was born and raised in Paducah and loved it dearly. He never had the urge to live anywhere else. He met my mother, his wife of 61 years, during the 1937 flood, when he was hospitalized with pneumonia. She was a nurse's aide volunteer during that time. They married in December 1938. He told me that was the best thing that ever came out of the flood."

She continued, "I did not know for many years (as I guess most of Paducah did not know) that it was my father. The photo of the cow on the balcony became famous, but the individual who actually accomplished the feat was never mentioned. The photos appeared in the June 1937 *National Geographic*, were shown in the news clips in movie theaters and were featured in Paducah's historical books. I have prepared this (following story) in loving memory and as a lasting tribute to my father."

Incidentally, Jimmelyn was Paducah's Centennial Beauty

Queen in 1956. She was awarded a trip to Havana, Cuba. Then in 1958, while a senior in high school, she was selected the Paducah Jaycee Beauty Queen and won a trip to Miami, Florida.

THE STORY OF THE COW ON THE BALCONY

(As told by Jimmy Huston to his daughter, Jimmelyn)

November 1936

I was 22 years old in January of 1937 when the rains came. It all started with a big sleet storm and then it rained 16 days straight in that one month. I read later where Paducah got 17 1/2 inches of rain in January, an all-time record. The temperatures were in the thirties and snow and ice floated on the waters. Everything was wet and frozen. This was all before the present flood wall was built, and with all the rain that we were getting, and the water coming down to us from up river, where there were also record rainfalls, the river waters at Paducah began to rise. The Ohio River swelled to seven miles wide. In a day's time, the rising waters would travel a block. People were flooded out of their homes. Businesses were shut down. Furniture was floating all around. Cars were submerged and the tops could barely be seen. The current was swift and it was dangerous and you didn't know what was just under the water's surface, but I didn't think about that then, because I was 22 and thought I was going to live forever. Every day we went out in homemade johnboats looking for people who were trapped by the rising waters. Times were hard. Electricity went off and we cooked and heated on a wood/coal stove. We used coal oil lamps and candles for light. Drinking water was contaminated, and so it was brought to us in cans. We couldn't bathe; we couldn't wash clothes; and we slept in the same clothes for days on end.

I lived with my mother and my mother's sister in a big two-story house at 527 North Sixth Street in Paducah at that time. (It is still standing today.) I had a job at Unique Cleaners on North Sixth Street. I remember reading in the Paducah paper where it said that there was so much water in Cairo that the manhole covers were blowing off. A bunch of us guys loaded up in somebody's car and drove over to see that. What a sight!

My mother's brother, Frank Lassiter, lived on "A" Street between Guthrie Avenue and 21st Street. He worked at the icehouse at Union Station. One day Uncle Frank called me and asked if I would go to his house and pick up his milk cow, Bossie, because he was stranded at work by the flood waters and the water was coming up at his home. Our home was on higher ground at the time, and the floodwaters had not reached us yet. Bossie was a dark brown milk cow that my Uncle Frank had owned for quite a while.

So, of course, I said I would, and I started out walking. By that time, you couldn't drive around much because you didn't know which streets were closed to high water. I got to his house and tied a rope on Bossie's halter, picked up a sack of feed, and the cow and I walked back to my house. That night I put her in the old wood garage we had out behind the house. Within a short period of time, the floodwaters reached our street and the ground was soggy. I knew I was going to have to move Bossie to higher ground, because I had heard that if she stood in wet ground for very long, her hooves would get soft and rot, so I put her on the back porch of the house. It was a big back porch with lattice around it. Gradually, the waters kept rising around our house and began to lap up to our porches. We started stacking furniture in the house and moving other furniture upstairs to the second floor. Of course my biggest problem was what was I going to do with Bossie? She gave us milk and I couldn't leave her where she was and we didn't know anyone out in the west end of town (which was still dry) who could take her. We also had about a dozen chickens that we didn't want anything to happen to. In those times, people kept live chickens that they would kill and eat. I finally decided that if everybody was going to move to the second story of the house, then Bossie and the chickens could move up there, too. I don't remember my mother's reaction to my idea, but I know what my reaction would have been if my sons had come to me with a hairbrained scheme like that. But when you're young, anything is doable.

Along about that time, we had approximately 20 people staying at the house with us. They were friends that had been flooded out and had to leave their homes. Of course, no one was working because the businesses were shut down. Everybody was doing some type of volunteer work. A lot of people had been moved to temporary makeshift shelters further out of town and volunteers were needed to cook for these displaced people and work the hospitals. I was cooking at George Rogers Clark Elementary School, which was one of the temporary shelters that had been set up. I also was going out with others in boats to pick people up and bring them in to higher ground. One of the people staying with us was a 78-year-old man I knew from work (but can't remember his name now). He had no family and so we took him in. The day came when he and I decided to move Bossie. We led Bossie off the lattice porch and in the back door of the house, through the kitchen and the hallway, and in to the front of the house where the steps were located that went to the second floor. She came into the house willingly and never balked a time. The steps were laid out so that you walked straight up 8 or 10 steps, then there was a landing, and then you made a right turn and went 8 or 10 steps more, up to the second floor. After we got Bossie in the house and to the first set of steps, she refused to budge. She would not step up on that first step. The old man pulled on the rope and I pushed on her back end. She would just "wall" her eyes and stretch her neck out while he was pulling and I was pushing, and not move at all. Of course, everybody in the house was standing around watching this effort and offering all kinds of verbal help. After about 15 minutes of me pushing and him pulling, we saw that was not going to work, but I got another idea. I told the old fella to go on up the steps as far as the rope would let him, and to stand clear. I told him, "This cow is going up those steps and once she gets started, she's not going to stop, so you need to stand clear and watch out for yourself." I didn't want him getting tromped by an "out-of-control" cow. So he moved on up the stairs and I grabbed hold of Bossie's tail and "crimped" it pretty hard. When I did that, she bellowed out in pain and flew up the stairs. I remember seeing the old man scrambling to get out of the way. She took the landing and the second set of steps without ever slowing down and never stopped until she reached the second floor. It was a comical thing to see. When we all got through laughing, we walked her through the second floor and through the outside front door, which opened out to the second story porch balcony. We didn't have to tie her or anything. Where was she going to go?

We next brought up her feed, and the chickens, and hauled buckets of coal and put all of it on the second story balcony to stay dry. So now all the animals were literally "high and dry!" The house was a two-family dwelling, so the second story had a bathroom and a small kitchen alcove, and we could still cook after we moved up there. We had chicken cooked every way imaginable and, of course, we had fresh milk and eggs.

A couple of weeks after I put Bossie on the balcony, I came down with double pneumonia and was put in the hospital. I stayed there approximately three weeks. While there, I was tended to by a very attractive, young, volunteer nurse's aide, who made quite an impression on me; so much so, that I married her in December of 1938 and we are still together today after almost 62 years. We have four children, three grandchildren, two great-grandchildren, and one great-great-grandchild to show for those years.

While I was in the hospital, the water finally got so high that my family and everybody staying at the house were evacuated. They left behind everything they owned and went to shelters. During that time, the river finally crested at 60.8 feet, the highest ever recorded.

As for Bossie, they left her there. The Coast Guard came by boat every day and milked her and made sure she had fresh hay and feed. The waters receded while I was gone and my Uncle Frank came and took Bossie home. He never told me if he had a hard time getting her down the stairs. If he did, I'm sure it wasn't near as difficult for him, or as painful for her. I will say that her tail never looked quite the same - - kinda hung at an angle, you might say. I have since seen three different photos taken of Bossie on that balcony. One of the photos was published in the June 1937 *National Geographic* magazine when they ran the story of the flood; another was published in several of the local books on Paducah's history. Bossie's predicament became famous not only on a local level, but elsewhere, and her pictures became symbols of the '37 flood for Paducah.

SINNOTT HOTEL, PADUCAH HARBOR PLAZA, 201 BROADWAY

Thishis old Paducah landmark began a new chapter in its long history with the final restoration work recently completed at a cost estimated to be around a half million dollars. Several hundred interested people attended a grand opening on October 12, 2001. Three of its five floors are luxury apartments of over 2,500 square feet, overlooking the Ohio River and downtown Paducah. The third and fourth floors have been leased to companies on a five-year plan. We understand there is a waiting list. The fifth floor penthouse is occupied by Bill and Meredith Schroeder, owners of the American Quilters Society building on Jefferson at 2nd Street. From their rooms are stairs leading to the roof garden. This area commands a beautiful panoramic view of the floodwall murals, the Ohio River, Owen's Island and South First Street.

The first floor is occupied by So Cool on Broadway, a nautical men's and women's clothing and accessory shop. The bed and breakfast rooms on the second floor are under the close attention and management of Beverly McKinley, innkeeper and owner. Beverly, a delightful lady, presides over the breakfasts when possible and becomes endeared to her guests by her ebullient, effervescent and outgoing nature. Featured is the Broadway Room, overlooking Paducah's Market House Museum, Second Street and the Ohio River. In addition to the Broadway Room, guests may choose to stay in the Harvest Moon Room, which includes a private bath and jacuzzi, the Hunt Room, which has a gas-burning fireplace, or the Lighthouse Room. All of these beautiful rooms are available for rental on a daily and weekly basis.

This imposing five-story building, designed and constructed by noted Paducah architect A.L. Lasater, dominates the corner of Second and Broadway. From its humble beginnings around 1900 it was first known as the Lagamarcino Hotel, then in 1905 as the Belvedere. Louis Lagamarcino, who had operated the New Richmond House Bar, First and Broadway, since 1894, became the proprietor. In 1915 the Belvedere was leased to John Sinnott by owner James P. Smith. Sinnott's youngest son, Stuart, who had been manager of the Palmer House Hotel, became manager. After Sinnott took over the hotel, John Lagamarcino, who had been manager of the Palmer House cafeteria, became manager of the Sinnott cigar stand. John Sinnott intended to attract traveling businessmen to his new establishment on the room-only European plan, rather than according to the American plan, in which meals were part of the daily fee. Smith and Sinnott remodeled and refurbished the 330-room public accommodation, and to emphasize the changes, changed the name to the Sinnott Hotel. Sinnott continued to operate the hotel until 1932, by which time the Irvin Cobb Hotel at Sixth and Broadway and the Ritz Hotel at 22nd and Broadway had usurped much of the local patronage. For 13 years it was vacant. In the 1970s and '80s it was used for storage by the United Home Furniture business.

Beverly McKinley, who bought the Sinnott Hotel building

Beverly McKinley, owner of Harbor Plaza
Hotel, 2nd and Broadway

in 1986, was born in Belleville, Illinois, where her parents, William and Gloria Collis McKinley, still live. After she was graduated from Belleville Township West High School, she enrolled at Murray State University, Murray, Kentucky, where she obtained her MS and BS degrees. She taught school in Murray for two years before moving to Paducah. She credits Sam Futrell, owner of Fern Lake Campground, with encouraging her to move to Paducah. He told her, "If you want to make it in this area, you must move to Paducah."

She made the move in 1986 and secured employment with the Kentucky Department of Education and worked full-time as a teacher and hospitality coordinator at West Kentucky Vocational School at Paducah. Although she retired three years ago, she still works there two days a week. She has been a member of the Paducah Rotary Club since 1994.

When asked why she bought the old hotel building, she said she had always wanted to own rental property with five units, so in 1986 when she saw a sign in the front window that the building was for sale and had five floors, she made arrangements to buy it from Bill Shelton, who had used it for storage. She said former Mayor Gerry Montgomery was very helpful getting her through the acquisition, helping her get a matching grant through Paducah Main Street, a program to help revitalize the downtown. She received help from Paducah Bank and applied for an enrichment loan for downtown historic projects. Her parents and others suggested that she renovate the lower two floors first and finish the others later, a plan that she followed. For a short while she housed her family's antique cars on the ground floor, but when other rental opportunities arose, they were moved. Although the hotel and other properties take up most of her time, she is active in the Cancer Society, Paducah Main Street Growth and the Hospitality Association. And she takes off days here and there to enjoy swimming, riding her bike and maintaining her interest in old cars.

I admire her courage and vision in restoring this old wonderful landmark, as it had not been used to house people since the 1950s, then was vacant for about 12 years. There was a possibility that it might have suffered the fate of many other buildings by being demolished. But now, beautifully restored and enjoying good occupancy, it has become a productive asset that will most certainly encourage others to help restore our downtown and enhance its attractiveness to visitors.

INDUSTRIAL PLANTS IN PADUCAH

MAGNAVOX

There were more than 20 industrial plants in Paducah in the middle of the 1950s. Only a few remain today. One that was here from 1947 to 1961 was the Magnavox Company, with home offices in Fort Wayne, Indiana, which built a large plant at 1500 North Eighth Street. They employed almost 400 to manufacture loud speakers, radio and television component parts. They manufactured similar products for industrial purposes. They also made electro-mechanical devices for military and commercial use. One of their principal products was a 20-pound device called a radio compass adapter, called the brain of the aviation industry's automatic pilot. These were made under a contract Magnavox had with the U.S. Navy.

Making loudspeakers was a Paducah specialty. These were

made not only for Magnavox products, but for other makes as well. They were designed to go into Hammond, Conn and Wurlitzer organs and jukeboxes. The Magnavox payroll in 1956 was more than a million dollars. The value of their manufactured products was estimated at six million dollars. The plant, which was deeded to Paducah Junior College, contained 105,000 square feet of floor space. B.J. Krueger, who had been superintendent of the International Shoe Company here for nearly 22 years, was the first manager. Magnavox ceased operations here in 1961 after a series of labor problems, and decided it could not operate profitably in Paducah. The last manager here was Curtis Seward, who joined our Rotary Club and served as president in 1958-1959. In 1962, Magnavox sold the plant to C.T.S. (Chicago Telephone Supply), which manufactured electrical components, and moved Adrian Vaksik here from the home office. He remained as general manager until 1975, when Jim C. Tidwell replaced him. C.T.S also had labor problems and closed the plant in 1978. Today, the Hannan Supply Company occupies the North Eighth property.

MODINE

In 1946, the Modine Company of Racine, Wisconsin, was looking for a place to build a convector radiator plant, primarily to supply the Ford Motor Company. With the help of the Paducah Chamber of Commerce, they bought a site at 30th and Jackson streets, along the P&I railroad tracks. They had 33 years of successful operations here and employed from 425 to 550 people during their peak years. When they lost their contract with Ford Motor in 1980, they ceased operations and closed the Paducah plant. The property remained vacant for a few years, was used for a few years by a lumber distributing firm from Klamath Falls, Oregon, and at present is the location for Celebrity Freight Lines.

Joe McWaters, who lives a couple of blocks east of us on Buckner Lane, was product foreman at Modine for years until they closed. Joe and Patsy have been good friends for years since before this neighborhood was developed. James "Soup" Jennings was personnel manager at Modine for years until they closed. (I didn't know for years that his name was James.) Soup's wife Jule was an invoice clerk at Petter Supply during the years that I was office manager. Edmund Arant was a production worker and Irene Davis was a secretary at Modine. When they married, Irene had to quit, as company policy would not permit both to be employed. Irene came to work at Petter and was my secretary for years. When she left, Jule took her place. Petter Supply was a distributor for Modine unit heaters and other heating and cooling products made at their Racine plant.

PAST DISTRICT GOVERNORS OF PADUCAH ROTARY CLUB

The Rotary Club of Paducah was chartered in 1915 with fifty- five members. From its first year until 2001, there have been 85 presidents of the Paducah club. Two Paducahans have served as district governors: H.L Smith in 1946-1947 and Orrin Nat Dortch in 1956-1957.

H. L. SMITH

H.L. Smith, christened Horace Luther Smith, was born in Jackson, Tennessee, October 6,1891. At his dad's farm in Weakley County, Tennessee, he did about every farm task, from threshing wheat to sawing stove wood. His father, George Wester Smith, raised every kind of crop that would grow in the area - tobacco, corn, wheat, cotton and hay. His early model threshing machine was operated by ten horses. During his boyhood days, H.L recalls swimming in the creek on the farm, and catching small catfish. When he finished his elementary and high school education, his father offered him enough money to pay for a year at college or to have a horse and buggy. H.L went to college and said he had been in school ever since, except for his Army service in World War I.

Except for that first year, H.L earned every penny of the cost of his schooling. He got his first B.A. degree from Hall-Moody, a Baptist Institute in Martin, Tennessee. He received a B.S. at Peabody College in Nashville, Tennessee, and an M.A. degree from Columbia University. He served as principal of schools in Palmersville and Union City, Tennessee, from 1912 to 1917. In 1917 he enlisted in the U.S. Army and served for 17 months overseas with the 105th Engineers, 30th Division, responsible for installations of bridges, pontoons, repair of railroads and trestles, and all operations necessary to keep the Army on the move in the French and Belgian action areas.

He met his wife-to-be, Maude Wyman, while both were students at Hall-Moody College and had a "whirlwind" courtship for nine years, and married upon his return from overseas in 1919. They were married at her parents' home in Carlsbad, New Mexico, and he then returned to his job as superintendent at Sharon, Tennessee. Before he became superintendent of schools at Paducah, Kentucky, he held principalships at Trenton, and Paris, Tennessee. After nine years at Paris, he came to Paducah, where he remained for 14 years.

H.L. became interested in Rotary, which he described as his most beloved extra-curricular activity, while he was living in Paris, Tennessee. He served as president of both Paris and Paducah Rotary clubs and continued as a member for 30 years. He was elected as president of the Paducah club 1941-1942 and served at district governor in 1946-1947.

He became superintendent of Henderson, Kentucky schools and was a member of the Henderson Rotary Club from 1947 to 1953. From 1952 to 1971, he was a field representative for the U.S. Office of Education in Chicago.

He retired to St. Petersburg, Florida, and lived there until his death May 20, 1981. Two sons of the Smiths became naval lieutenants. Harry L, now retired in Colorado, was graduated from Purdue University, had special training in the technical field at Harvard, and saw considerable service as an officer in electronics and

H.L. Smith-
Superintendent,
Paducah Public Schools,
1933-1947; President,
Paducah Rotary,
1941-1942;
Rotary District
Governor, 1946-1947

radar in the Aleutians. Later he was connected with an atomic-electronic company near Boston. Thomas, the younger son, was graduated from Annapolis and served three years aboard the aircraft carrier "Midway." He resigned his commission, returned to college and was studying electronics and about to become a member of the MIT faculty, when he was recalled to active service aboard ship in the Mediterranean.

H.L Smith's lifelong interests were hunting, fishing, and camping, to which in his later years he added golf and photography.

(I am indebted to his son Harry, for very graciously furnishing me with this information, including an excellent photo. And, incidentally, I'm also grateful to Gene Katterjohn, Harry's classmate at Purdue and his good friend, for putting me in touch with Harry.)

ORRIN NAT DORTCH

rrin Nat Dortch was born to Nat F. and Martha Bell Bass
Dortch in Goodlettsville, Tennessee, in 1902. He attended
Vanderbilt University for three years, majoring in geology.
He worked a while in California as a geologist, then moved to
Henderson, Kentucky, and joined his father in the tobacco business
in the leaf department of W.S. Mathews and Sons. In 1927, he
became president of the company and moved the business to 1034
Kentucky Avenue, Paducah. He traveled extensively in Central
America and the West Indies until 1939. He supervised and operated the manufacturing equipment, and managed the marketing of the
product, furnishing leaf tobacco and several brands of chewing
tobacco to both domestic and foreign markets. He taught geology
at Paducah Community College for 25 years. A former student
named the Dorchii Fern, a fossil, in his honor. He was the founder
of the Big Rivers Area Geological Society and a member of the
Kentucky Geological Society.

He joined the Paducah Rotary Club in 1928, served at president in 1956-1957 and became a Paul Harris Fellow, the highest
honor in Rotary. He served as governor of Rotary District 671 in
1957-1958. He was very active in the leadership of the Four Rivers
Boy Scout Council and for several years was Scoutmaster of Scout
Troop #5 at the First Presbyterian Church at 7th and Jefferson
streets, where he was a member and taught Sunday school for many
years. A past chairman of the American Red Cross chapter and a
past coordinator of the local civil defense, he also served a term as
chairman of the Paducah Community Chest and worked with the
polio foundation.

Orrin Nat Dortch and his wife Jesse Weir Dortch had one
son, Orrin Nat Dortch, Jr. and two daughters Marion Dortch Rosser
of Lafayette, Indiana, and Jessiann Dortch McCarthy of Port
Matilda, Pennsylvania. Nat died at his home on North 36th Street,
Paducah, March 3, 1992 at the age of 90.

I have fond memories of Nat Dortch, who I first met while

A Young Man's Interests and Pursuits

Nat Dortch, Sr.

active in Scout Troop #5. He was a fine role model for the young boys in the troop and gave generously of his time, helping us learn the Scout rules and laws. He spent days with us at the two-week camps at Pakentuck, near Ozark, Illinois. In later years he was a good customer of my employer, the Petter Supply Company, and purchased many items he needed to keep his plant running. He was president of the Rotary Club of Paducah when I became a member in 1956. We made several trips together attending Rotary meetings and conferences in our West Kentucky district. We remained good close personal friends throughout his lifetime.

FRIENDSHIPS OVER THE YEARS

GOOD FRIENDS

ROY C. MANCHESTER

When I joined the Boy Scouts in 1926, Roy C. Manchester was Scout Executive. Scout headquarters was in the former YMCA building on the northeast corner of Sixth and Broadway. From my early days as a Tenderfoot Scout, thru the grades to Eagle Scout, at Scout camps, and through several years as Scoutmaster, Manchester, though a strict disciplinarian, was always kind, patient and supportive. Small in stature, he stood tall with all the Scouts and leaders who were involved in Scouting. We remained warm friends through the rest of his life. He served as Boy Scout executive from 1919 to 1953. He was executive secretary of the Paducah Rotary Club from 1926 until 1944. He was an elder emeritus of the First Presbyterian Church and served as superintendent of the Sunday school for 18 years. He served as manager of the Paducah-McCracken Airport for eight years and was manager of Mt. Kenton Cemetery from 1953 until 1970. He died in 1975 at age 87.

Manchester's wife Lou Esther and two sons, Charles and Robert, were also good friends. Esther, who was very active in the Paducah Women's Club, and in the Presbyterian Church, lived the last years of her life in the Irvin Cobb Apartments. She died July 18, 2000. She had been a member of the Paducah Women's Club since 1929, serving a term as president. She was a member of the

Daughters of the American Revolution and served as a Den Mother for Cub Scout Pack 23.

She was a volunteer for several civic organizations, including the American Cancer Society, the Market House Museum, the Paducah Symphony Orchestra and the Rotary Club. Their older son, Charles, a talented cellist, moved back to Paducah and joined the Paducah Rotary Club in 1981. He has written the club bulletin for many years and is a Paul Harris Fellow. He recently retired as director of the Paducah Symphony and was manager of the Market House Museum for a number of years.

Their other son, Bob, is an experienced and well-known practicing attorney and served as chairman of the Paducah Zoning Board for a number of years.

SAM LIVINGSTON

Sam Livingston was an upper classman when I entered Augusta Tilghman High School in February of 1927. (Ours was the last class to enter as freshmen). Sam began writing for the *Paducah Sun-Democrat* while in high school and in 1929, as a 17-year-old, fresh out of Tilghman, became the paper's first sports editor. He was elected treasurer of his sophomore class and was on the staff of the *West Kentucky Bell*, the school newspaper that year, and became editor in 1928-1929. He was elected to the National Honor Society in his senior year.

In 1926, while attending my first Boy Scout camp, at Dixon Springs, Illinois, he was my tent leader. We had a difference of opinion about the proper method of holding the tent flaps up in a folded position during daylight hours. I wanted to use blanket pins, which I had brought for that purpose, while Sam would allow only wooden forks we had to make from limbs. A wrestling match between us did not settle the issue, but when Scout Executive Roy Manchester reminded me that we were required to accept the discipline from our leaders, I agreed and we became good friends.

When I belonged to the Paducah Jaycees (Junior Chamber

of Commerce) from 1935-1949, we attended meetings and conventions together. During the long tenure of Ralph McRight as Tilghman football coach, Sam would invite me to be on his weekly radio "Quarterback Club" program to quiz the coach after the games. When the Jaycees started the promotion and construction of the Edwin J. Paxton Municipal Golf Course in 1940, we were involved to some degree in the details and work. Sam became an ardent golfer and was always on the course weekends. He had his own foursome, but we played together now and then. In 1939 Sam, Edward Scott, W.L. Beasley and I drove to California to attend the Rose Bowl parade and football game. It was the first trip west for all of us, as I remember, and we thoroughly enjoyed the experience of seeing new parts of the country. Edgar Bergen was grand marshal of the parade, which we enjoyed from good seats secured for us by Will Scott, Ed's uncle and a California newspaperman. Before the New Year's game we took in a lot of the sights and were fascinated by the beautiful flowers and the pageantry of the festivities. One day three of us took in a golf exhibition in the Los Angeles Coliseum that featured many of the prominent golfers of the time. W.L Beasley did not go with us, but instead went for a visit to Forest Lawn Cemetery.

During World War II, Sam joined the Navy and served until the war's end. While stationed at San Diego he met and married a delightful girl, Loretta. After leaving the service Sam and Loretta moved to Paducah. In the second leg of his 48th year with the newspaper, he and Editor Edwin J Paxton Jr. started WKYB radio in 1946, then later added WKYC-FM. In 1957 they sold the radio stations and started WPSD-TV. Sam was station manager until he retired in 1977 at age 65. Then, as we understand, by an agreement he had with Loretta, they moved to Hercules, California. Sam died there at the age of 80, December 1992, and was buried in Temple Israel Cemetery in Paducah.

John D. Williams, who became his successor at the TV station, said, "There has never been a guy quite like him. He was one of a kind. He was a perfect gentleman with good morals, the utmost integrity and the respect of everyone he came in contact with." Tom Butler, who worked for Livingston for 15 years at the station, said he was probably Tilghman's number one football fan while he was here. Fred Paxton, who worked with Sam beginning in 1961, after serving as associate editor of the *Sun-Democrat*, said Sam was very popular with all the people at NBC Television and worked very closely with network officials.

JOHN WRIGHT POLK, JR

I became acquainted with John Wright Polk when we both lived on Harahan Boulevard in 1929. John was the only son of John and Martha Anderson Polk. His older sister Martha was in my brother Harry's school class, and his sister Barbara, was several years younger than John. They lived on the southwest corner of Harahan and Harrison Street. I lived in the middle of the 300 block. Most of the other boys in the neighborhood were high school age and played games together in the several vacant lots close by. Although younger and smaller, John would occasionally join in.

During my last two years at Pakentuck Boy Scout camp in Illinois, John was there in a cabin next to our "big boys" cabin, which was set at the highest point on the hill. We went on hikes together and swam and participated in the games and activities with those in our group. John graduated from Augusta Tilghman High School in 1935 and was a 1938 graduate of Paducah Junior College. He played the trumpet in the Tilghman band and continued his interest in music for many years. He played with a number of local bands, including Harry Ware and Jack Staulcup's. Later he formed his own band and played for dances for many clubs and dance pavilions all around the area. World War II saw us going our separate ways for almost a decade.

When he opened a shoe store at 312 Broadway, I would stop in to see him frequently. By then he had married Joanne Jones and had built a home on North 36th Street. During the years 1952 to 1959 we performed together in the Charity League Follies and enjoyed the practices and afterwards. In the middle fifties, he became Paducah manager for the Kentucky Mortgage Company, and then later moved to Lexington, Kentucky, to become vice president of the loan production department. In 1973 at the request of Kentucky Governor Wendell Ford, he set-up the Kentucky Housing Corporation and was director until 1978. He returned to Paducah after working for 20 years in Lexington. Ill health forced him to retire a few years after his return. He died February 17,1993, and was survived by Joanne; two daughters, Ann Elwyn Gray of Louisville, and Sue Berry Dickerson of Paducah; two sons, John W. Polk of Somerset and David Anderson Polk of Paducah, one sister, Barbara Woosley of Huntsville, Alabama; and nine grandchildren. He was a member, vestryman and warden of Grace Episcopal Church in Paducah.

John loved life and always lived it to the fullest. He was in his element at parties and gatherings of all kinds and occasions. He knew everybody and was very popular with all his friends. He greeted everyone with a warm and ready smile and always seemed to enjoy life. To me, he was a delightful and warm-hearted friend.

JIMMIE YELTEMA

I don't remember if I first met Jimmie at school or at Scout camp. We were in the same class and as our last names were at the end of the alphabet, we were always assigned seats on the back row. It had its good points - we were overlooked when mischief occurred, being hidden from view of the teacher. And the bad points included being ignored when we raised our hands to answer questions, as there were too many hands up on the front rows. We usually took the same subjects during the last two school years. At camp we were in the same cabin or tent, did projects and athletic events together. After our junior school year we pooled our money and bought the old Scout camp 1923 model Dodge for $15 from Scoutmaster Roy Manchester. Jimmie, who was a pretty good jack-of-all-trades, got me to help him put new piston rings in the engine. When camp was over, we drove it home, or at least intended to. It quit on us at

Vienna, Illinois, within 25 miles from home. We hitchhiked from there and Jimmie got friend Marvin Howard to tow him back to his house. Jimmie and I painted it with Tilghman blue and white, and Jimmie drew a picture of a football player on each side. The first week we had it home, a back tire blew and we scrounged around town and finally found one for $1 that would fit at Otto Gross's junkyard at Second and Jefferson streets.

Jimmie had a canoe that we used to paddle up and down the Ohio River. He wanted me to accompany him on a canoe trip up the Ohio to Louisville, but I had to work for Dad and could not go. So he took off one summer day and got as far as the mouth of the Tradewater, which he mistook for the Ohio, and after paddling half a day discovered his mistake. Discouraged, he paddled back home.

We were on the high school track team together for two years. The first year, we both ran the 110-yard low hurdles. The last year I ran the 110 and 220-yard dashes. We won about half of the time.

After high school, Jimmie was the night watchman for the Palmer House; a job he acquired when his uncle retired. He lived with his aunt and uncle, his parents having died when he was very young. His aunt worked for years at Wahl's Laundry at 10th and Kentucky Avenue. They lived in a small cottage near the corner of Sixteenth and Madison streets, a few doors from my father's number 3 grocery. A few years later Jimmie went to work for VanAart Florist at Sixth and Broadway. The VanAarts lived on the northeast corner of Sixteenth and Madison, two doors from Jimmie. Jimmie worked there for the rest of his life, continuing after Bob Cherry bought the florist business. Jimmie was known as one of the best floral designers in town.

During our 50th high school class reunion in 1981, Jimmie made the table decorations and was a big help to the committee in getting things together. Jimmie first married his high school sweetheart, Virginia Usher, and they had one daughter, Judy. They divorced after a number of years, and then he married Beatrice Harrison, a widow. Jimmie died at home May 2,1985 and was buried in the Kansas Cemetery near Melber, Kentucky.

HARRY J. LIVINGSTON

I first knew Harry J. Livingston in 1930, when we both attended Boy Scout camp at Pakentuk, Illinois. Then a few years later he became a member of the Von Baron Ironclad Fraternity, a group of high school boys who ran around together until World War II broke up "that ole gang of mine." Harry, who was always known then as "HJ," was a cousin of Sam Livingston. H.J. and his brother Lee lived on Jefferson Street, just west of the Illinois Central Hospital, around the corner from Harahan Boulevard. Lee was graduated from Tilghman High School a year before I was.

Harry graduated from Tilghman in 1937 and worked at M. Livingston Company during his teen years, until the draft was instituted in 1940. His name was among the first drawn in McCracken County. He was sent to Ft. Thomas, Kentucky. In June 1942, he married Gloria Walker, who had moved to Paducah in 1936. Also, that June he was transferred to Ft. Campbell, Kentucky, and was commissioned a second lieutenant in April 1943. He was stationed at Tinker Field, Oklahoma, and Sandia Air Force Base, Albuquerque, New Mexico and then was sent to Europe, where he served until the war ended. I saw him once while overseas when he visited me in France one day.

Harry returned to Paducah in November 1945, the same month as I did. I had resumed work at Petter Supply and was traveling in Tennessee when I next saw Harry. He and Gloria had moved to Dyersburg, Tennessee, bought a doughnut-making machine and were furnishing doughnuts to all the eating places in town. Then on another trip through there a few months later, I learned they had bought a ladies' hat shop on the square, from a woman who was retiring. They were doing well. After a short while Harry was recalled as a regular officer in the Air Force and I lost track of him. When he and Gloria came back here to live in 1973, I soon learned of his activities during the intervening 28 years.

Harry had a very interesting Air Force career. He had attained the rank of captain and was stationed at Elgin AFB, Florida;

Scott AFB, Illinois; Arnold Development Center, Tullahoma Tennessee; USAFE Headquarters, Weisbaden, Germany; and lastly Lowry AFB, Denver. The family, now grown to four with the addition of daughters, Stanlee and Gail, joined him on every assignment. At Weisbaden, he was executive director to the commanding officer and handled all air transportation under the command of General William Turner. During his final six years at Lowry, he was special assistant to three generals. He received recognition as the outstanding Colorado citizen of 1959 for his work with city leaders. On June 30, 1962, Harry retired as a lieutenant colonel. He received 13 awards, including five stars and three commendation ribbons.

After retirement, Harry worked four years for REA Express in Denver as sales director of eleven states. He moved to St. Louis in 1966 to manage Midwest Cigar Company, a subsidiary of M. Livingston. He came home to Paducah and rejoined M. Livingston. Through his contacts in St. Louis, he brought Timex into the business in 1975 and the company became the fourth largest distributor of Timex in the country. He supervised the Timex division for twelve years and retired for good in 1987.

He served as president of the Paducah Country Club for four years. During his tenure, a new clubhouse was built on Holt Road. He served a term on the Paducah Power System Board. He and Gloria were members of First Baptist Church, where he was a charter member of the Chapel Bible Class. Every year, Harry invited all members of the Von Baron Club he could locate to a dinner at the Country Club. Among those were Ray Strittmatter, Cleve Townsend, Bob Cherry, Paul Martin, Richard (Buster) Blackston, John R. Anderson and me. On other occasions when old friends came to town, he would call a few of us to meet for dinner with them. He continued to stay in touch with his multitude of friends by phone, a trait that was typical of him throughout his adult life. He was in contact with people he had known since high school days. If you wanted to learn what happened to an old mutual friend, you would ask Harry and he probably knew. Harry died August 18, 2001 after being confined to his home by illness for the last few years. He was buried at Temple Israel Cemetery, Paducah, with services conducted by Dr. Kevin McCallon and the Reverend Robert Kersey of First Baptist Church.

WALTER LIPSCOMB BEASLEY, JR.

This book would not be complete without the inclusion of a story about Walter L. "Dub" Beasley, one of my closest and dearest friends since teenage years. Although he is three years younger and was not in school with me, he and I soon became acquainted through tennis, canoeing, the Jaycees, photography and other mutual interests and pursuits. We spent many hours together on the tennis courts at Barkley Park, now the site of the Executive Inn. Some of my favorite pictures are those we took together, which have preserved happy memories of our young days.

In 1939 we drove to Pasadena, California, to attend the Rose Bowl Parade and football game with Sam Livingston and Ed Scott. Since this was our first trip west, driving through Texas, New Mexico, Arizona and California, was a very impressionable trip for us. After World War II we became closer friends. We were both single and we ran around together, double-dated frequently together, and one year flew to New York together to take in a Broadway show, to see the sights there, and then ride the train to Franklin Field, Philadelphia, Pennsylvania, to attend the Army-Navy football game.

Dub married Jessie Hibbitts in 1951. Jessie, a native of Pikeville, Kentucky, had moved to Paducah a few years earlier to do social work after graduating from Berea College, Berea, Kentucky. I was pleased to serve as his best man at the ceremony in Pikeville. There were no interstate highways at that time, so I made it a leisurely two-day drive to get there, and made an overnight stop at Russellville, Kentucky, to visit former Paducahan, Oscar McCutcheon and his wife, who owned a florist shop there. I had just bought a new yellow Mercury convertible from Farrington Motors and enjoyed the drive with the top down as I navigated the winding roads and "S" curves in the hills of eastern Kentucky on my way to Pikeville, which is about 20 miles from the West Virginia border.

After Zelma Nicholson and I were married in 1957, we resumed going out together as couples. Then when Ed and Joan Hank moved back to Paducah from Smithland, where he ran a Hank Hardware store, the six of began to get together for each birthday and anniversary. We have always enjoyed being together and watching our children grow and become adults. Ed died in July 2001, but we remaining five continue to observe past traditions.

Dub was graduated from Tilghman, class 1935, and worked for Lockheed Aircraft before Pearl Harbor, when he volunteered for the Air Corps and was commissioned a second lieutenant. He saw service in New Guinea, Okinawa and Japan, piloting C-47 aircraft. He returned home afterward with the rank of captain, retained his commission in the Air Force Reserve and retired after 20 years with the rank of major. Dub was active in the family business, Beasley Marble & Granite Company for about sixty years, designing and selling monuments. When he wasn't working, he spent countless hours touring cemeteries all over the country, visiting and photographing graves of renowned people. He is especially fascinated by epitaphs and has published a book of his collection entitled *The Bottom Line*. Dub sold the business in 1998 and is now retired.

His hobby of photographing tombstones led him to discover that the grave of seismologist Charles F. Richter in California had never been marked. So he supplied an appropriate monument and had it engraved, "He devised the scale by which the magnitude of earthquakes is measured." Dub's interest in Paducah's history had led him to be active in preserving a number of Paducah's landmarks. He had a leading role in preserving the 3,500-pound city hall clock bell. He assisted Gene Katterjohn, who moved the historic horse drinking fountain at Tenth and Broadway back to the grass plot out of traffic. His interest in fine stonework started in the restoration project for the Carnegie Library fountain, which was dismantled about 30 years ago, carted off to Judge David Reed's property on old Mayfield Road, where it remained until 1994 when Dub's sponsors, Ed Hank and Gene Katterjohn, had it reconstructed by Crawford Enterprises and erected on Jefferson Street between 24th and 25th. His interest in Paducah culture and history is still active today.

SAM S. SLOAN

According to old records and from details furnished by his son, Monroe, Sam Sloan was born while his family lived near 5th and Jackson streets. He remembers the old Fred Kamleiter grocery in his neighborhood. That was his world until he was older, and on holidays and Sundays, would ride the streetcars into Paducah and out to Wallace Park in Arcadia to watch baseball games and other attractions there. Sam's father, Louis B. Sloan, described as a dignified man with a goatee, was born in Germany, came to America as a young man, landed in New York and came west to Paducah. He became a peddler, and with a pack on his back, he traveled all over West Kentucky and Southern Illinois, selling trinkets, needles, thimbles, combs, and other items that people could not buy without making a trip to the city. Later he peddled dry goods by horse and wagon.

(The Paducah city directory of 1894 lists a Louis Sloninsky, peddler, living at 908 Jackson. The only Sloan family listed, Abram and Elizabeth, lived at 319 Norton Street, Also listed is Fred Kamleiter's grocery at 437-441 South Third Street.)

Sam quit school at age 15. He carried papers for the *Morning Register* and the *Evening Sun*, which later became the *Sun-Democrat*. Later, he went to work for S. Fels and Brothers Dry Goods company at 4th and Jefferson streets, which became Rubel's Dry Goods. In 1908 at age 18, he went on the road for Rubel and traveled northern Mississippi. In 1913, he and his brother Mert went into the grocery business, first at 13th and Monroe, then 5 years later at the northeast corner of 12th and Jefferson in an existing building owned by the Overstreet family. Known as Sloan Brothers, the business grew and prospered. They became part of the Piggly-Wiggly chain and developed seven stores in Paducah, Murray and Mayfield, serving all of them out of the Jefferson Street store. They continued to operate until March 1929 when they sold out.

The Sloan Brothers store was familiar to me, as it was the nearest grocery to my father's grocery that opened in 1923 at 621

Broadway. When we came here, there were over 100 "mom & pop" groceries in Paducah in neighborhoods all over town, but Sloan's was the most prominent. They sold on credit and delivered. We were "cash & carry."

Sam entered the insurance field and became district manager of the Southwest Mutual Insurance Company, a position he held for more than thirty years. He maintained an office in the ten-story Citizens Bank building and was very visible downtown, as he walked up and down the street, meeting and greeting everyone he passed. The wave of his hand, his wide smile and booming voice became his trademarks. His secretary sent out birthday cards to customers and others, written in a bold and neatly scripted hand. His entry into Paducah civic work apparently started in 1920. He had become involved in a number of civic and charitable causes and by the mid-thirties, was secretary and treasure of six organizations at the same time. Although he was never a Scout, he was treasurer of the Four Rivers Boy Scout Council for ten years. And although never a member of the Junior Chamber of Commerce (which didn't start here until he was over the age limit), he was awarded an honorary life membership. Sam was one of the first workers for the Community Chest, a movement that started in 1932. He helped organize the Lions Club in Paducah, served as president in 1926-'27, was secretary for 20 years, served a year as district governor in 1937 and was a member for fifty years. He was very active in the Salvation Army and a life member of their advisory board. He was a fifty-year member of the Elks Club and served as Exalted Ruler in 1923,1926 and 1957. He was a regular worker for the Red Cross and helped find shelter for thousands of stranded Paducahans during the 1937 flood. He was active in the Paducah Shrine club, was elected president in 1952 and was a leader in the Scottish Rite club and was a 32nd Degree Mason. Sam was instrumental in bringing Kitty League baseball to Paducah, and was a strong supporter of Brooks Stadium. He helped organize the Toastmasters Club, wrote the weekly bulletin and served a term as president. For 11 years, he was chairman of the Easter Seal Campaign, which raised money for crippled children. He helped organize the Greater Paducah Association, which later became the Greater Paducah Chamber of Commerce. He was a member of Temple Israel, was past president of its brotherhood and headed the congregation.

November 29, 1960 was SAM SLOAN DAY in Paducah, as grateful Paducahans paid tribute to a man who was called Paducah's greatest civic leader. The event took place at the Irvin Cobb Hotel with a joint meeting of the Lions and Rotary clubs and with prominent members of all the civic and service clubs in attendance. Among the tributes were: A Duke of Paducah Award by Mayor Robert Cherry, a Kentucky Colonel award by Bert Combs, Governor of the Commonwealth of Kentucky, a Life Time Membership award by the Shrine Club of Paducah, and a Life Membership award in the Paducah Lions Club. Members of the organizations he had served spoke of his contributions made over the past four decades.

For the last ten years of his life, he was agent-emeritus of his firm. He died in January 1970, after a short illness. He was buried in Temple Israel Cemetery. Rabbi Max Kaufman officiated at the service.

ROLLIE BARTLETT

Rollie Bartlett was born in Paducah in 1916. He graduated from Reidland High School in 1934, and was in school with my brother-in-law and sister-in-law, Rex Nicholson and Katherine Nicholson Flowers, and they were good friends. Rollie lived on Farley on Paducah's south side, rode the bus to school, and occasionally had dinner at the Nicholson home, a few doors from the school.

I met Rollie a few years after I was employed by Henry A. Petter Supply. Rollie was a water meter repairman for the Paducah Water Company, and had a repair shop in their plant at First and Washington streets, across from Maiden Alley, behind the Petter warehouse. I became acquainted with him as he made trips to our salesroom to pick up supplies.

In September 1943, he volunteered for the U.S. Army Aviation Engineers, attended basic training with the 883rd A/B Engineer Battalion at Westover Field, Massachusetts; took post basic training at Bradley Field, Connecticut, and at the Air Force Base, Richmond, Virginia. He was attached to the 14th Air Force in China, and was sent throughout bases in the theater, designing, improvising, building and maintaining pressure type water filter systems. When the war was over, he was sent to Shanghai to restore water service to the Air Base at Kiangwan. He was discharged in February 1945 with tech 5 rank, and was awarded the EAME and APCM medals with 2 bronze stars.

Rollie went back to his former job at the Paducah Water Company and was made superintendent of distribution. When I returned to the Petter office in 1949, after traveling for four years, I made frequent trips to Rollie's office soliciting business, as municipal water departments were my main area of responsibility. Rollie had married Laurine Wood in 1941 and they had a son, Rollie Brent. We visited infrequently and enjoyed eating out together.

Rollie and I were members of the West Kentucky Chapter of the Water Works Operators Association for over forty years, and oftimes would travel together to attend their meetings. And we would get together with our wives at the annual meetings of the West Kentucky-West Tennessee Water Works Association, held alternately in Kentucky and Tennessee, in Louisville, Lexington, Knoxville, Nashville or Memphis.

After Laurine died in June 1969, we continued getting together now and then. One evening when Zelma's long-time friend, Velda Robertson, was staying with our children while we went out to eat with Rollie, he became interested in Velda and they were married in 1973. We have maintained our close relationship ever since.

Rollie has been interested in baseball all his life. He spent a lot of his leisure hours as a kid, playing pick up games. He was seldom without a ball, bat and glove. He watched games at old Hook's Park during the Kitty League era, games at Brooks Park, and wherever baseball was played. He loved every aspect of the game and always had a baseball story to relate. He could tell you who played where. I suspect he spent many hours watching (and dozing) in front of the TV screen. He has met many big league players personally. For ten years he sponsored and managed Khouri League teams. For a number of years they owned a home at Anna Maria Island, Florida, and spent winters there. Rollie, a loyal supporter of the St. Louis Cardinals, always enjoyed going to their training sessions in Florida and usually stayed until spring training was over. We visited with them several times there. They sold the place when they found driving back and forth was too much for them. After he retired in 1973, Rollie was chairman of the Paducah-McCracken Senior Citizens for ten years.

Rollie and Velda are dear friends and knowing them has enriched our lives.

THE ROMEOS

Members: Ed Hank, Gene Katterjohn, Bob Cherry, Barron White, Jim Hardy, John Hornsby, P.J. Grumley, Jimmie Rieke and Elmer Breidert. Associates: Louis Myre, Bill Howerton, and Henry Whitlow. The Lunch-Bunch meets weekly on Friday. They called themselves the "Romeo's," (Retired Old Men Eating Out).

This began in 1982, when two or more of us would try to get together for lunch. It might be any day of the week. More often than not, one of us would be unable to go due to business or a prior commitment. Many weeks we simply could not get together the same day. Finally, it was decided that we would make Friday our special day and try to avoid conflicts. We all set aside that day, thus making it unnecessary to call around and make arrangements. This plan worked well and we began to look forward to our meetings. We have become very close friends. Most members were near retirement age when we started. And now all who remain no longer work. We have lost some, including Jim Hardy, Jim Rieke, Bob Cherry, Ed Hank and John Hornsby. We are of different backgrounds and life experiences, but hold similar beliefs and philosophies.

We met at a number of places, at first most frequently at Kountry Kastle on Clarks River Road, owned and operated by Max Edwards. When some of us had commitments that limited our time, we met downtown at Moss Rose Cafe or Gold Rush Corner. Over the years we have met at a number of different places, including the Holman House, at the mall at Steak & Shake, Damon's and Back Yard Burger. Recently, we have met a few times at the American Legion Hall on Legion Drive. There have been Fridays when only two of us were in town or able to get together.

As we meet together for a little over a hour each week, we've never had enough time to solve the world's problems, but like many other local groups that gathered together over coffee or a meal, we have enjoyed the fellowship and opportunity to voice and share our views on current events.

GUS ED HANK

Ed Hank was one of my best and closest friends. Although he was seven years my junior, we were friends since we became adults. Our spouses were also the best of friends and for years

Katterjohn, Hank, Cherry

we four observed birthdays and anniversaries together, along with Jessie and W.L. Beasley, who are close friends. Ed was a fourth generation owner of the Hank Bros. Hardware Company, now enjoying its 102nd year in Paducah. Sons Chuck and Jim now own and manage the business.

Ed Hank was graduated from the University of Kentucky and then was inducted into the U.S. Army. Upon graduation from the Infantry School at Fort Benning, Georgia, as a lieutenant, he was sent to Germany in October 1944 with the 78th Infantry Division. He fought in the Battle of the Hurtgen Forest, the Battle of the Bulge and the Rhineland campaigns, was wounded and received the Purple Heart. Other decorations were the Combat Infantry Badge, Silver Star, Bronze Star and three Battle Stars. Released as a captain, he returned home to enter the family business. He married Joan Ferguson in 1950. In addition to sons Chuck and Jim, who now operate the family business, they had a son Gus E. Hank IV, who at age 16 drowned in the Ohio River. A track award and scholarship fund were established at Tilghman High School in his memory.

Hornsby, White, Hardy

In 1962 Ed was called back to active duty with the 100th Infantry Division for one year during the Cuban and Berlin crises. He returned to the family business and operated three stores - one downtown, one in Lone Oak and one on the South Side.

Ed was a past president of the Kentucky Hardware Association and served on the boards of the Salvation Army, Senior Citizens, Lourdes, Main Street, and the Paducah Area Transit System. He was an Eagle Scout, a past commander of American Legion Post 31, and of Chapter 585, Military Order of the Purple Heart. The Paducah Chamber of Commerce named him 1995 Citizen of the Year. In 2000, he was selected Veteran's Day Parade Marshal. We got together in France in 1994 for the memorial service at the U.S. Military Cemetery at Coulterville, Omaha Beach, in observance of the 50th anniversary of D-Day, World War II.

Gus Ed Hank III died at home July 24, 2001 at age 79, after battling cancer for almost a year. He and I were the first of the Romeos and met for lunch on Fridays since 1982. In the 2002 Wall to Wall calendar, the tribute to him reads, "Gus Ed Hank was admired for his benevolence and charitable kindness He wore his Paducah pride with honor and personal satisfaction. His devotion to his family and this community has made Paducah a much better place to live and raise our families. He was a wonderfully positive influence in our community. We will always member him with much joy, a real hero." (Amen)

ROBERT C. CHERRY

Bob Cherry and I were long-time good friends. When we were members of the Von Baron Iron Clad Fraternity, we were together at the regular meetings at the clubhouse we built on the Blandville Road. Like most boys who grew up in the Depression years of the 1930s, we had very little money to spend and saved up for the weekend activities. Bob was working at VanAart Florist and was their top salesman and sold more corsages at Easter than all the others. Jimmy Yeltema, floral designer for VanAart's, asked the

Grumley, Katterjohn, Cherry

owners to hire me during the Easter rush and I worked there several pre-Easter Saturdays printing addresses on the corsage boxes. We worked all day Saturday and Saturday night until early Sunday morning. There were about ten of us there to make and get out the flowers before the Sunday services. Deliveries started several hours before daylight, requiring a flashlight, in some cases, to identify house numbers. The boys I remember were John and Charles Bryan, Ray Stewart and John Iler. Iler helped me with boxes and also helped with deliveries. He told me recently that Bill Ryan, Bill Black, and Charles Humphries were also there some years. Around midnight Mrs. VanAart served a table-full of sandwiches and drinks. It was a crowded, busy place, and there was a lot of laughing and joking. It was fun and we were having a ball. Cherry was everywhere, making sure things went smoothly. He bought out the VanAart's in 1946 and it became a very successful company.

He served three terms as mayor of Paducah, 1952-56, 1960-1964, and 1968-1972. He was 1963 national president of the FTD Association, a worldwide floral delivery service, and became president of Inter Flora, the international florist organization in 1967. As world president, he traveled to many foreign countries, including Vatican City, where he had a private audience with Pope Pius XII. In 1993, at the urging of City Commissioner John Hornsby, the commission named the civic center on Park Avenue, the Robert C. Cherry Civic Center.

Bob graduated from Tilghman High School in 1935. At the 50th class reunion, he was asked what was his "best time." His response was, "The time with the Von Barons." Bob served in the Army in 1942, as first sergeant in the 101st Airborne engineers, and participated in the invasions of Iwo Jima and Okinawa. When World War II correspondent Ernie Pyle was killed during the invasion of Iwo Jima, Bob made his grave blanket of cycas leaves and native flowers. Pyle's body was later buried in Punch Bowl Cemetery in Hawaii. Bob was past president of the Paducah Jaycees, the Paducah Kiwanis Club, and the Kentucky Municipal League. He was a faithful member of the First Baptist Church and served as an usher for years, greeting his many friends as they arrived. Bob married Lynne McKenney in 1944. They had two children, Robert Cherry Jr. of Paducah, and Dana Cherry Johnson of Baltimore, Maryland. Bob was one of the original members of the Romeos. We would decide where to eat, then drive individually and meet. Later after Bob had a stroke and it was hard for him to drive, Ed Hank began picking him up. This was done for him the rest of his life. Bob died July 9, 1995. Services were held at the First Baptist Church. His former pastor, John Wood, came from Texas to conduct the service. He was buried in Maple Lawn Cemetery.

JAMES CALHOUN RIEKE II

Jim was a lifelong friend. We were both members of Boy Scout Troop #5 at the Presbyterian Church. We attended several Scout camps together and in the late 1920s were cabin mates at Camp Pakentuck, near Ozark, Illinois. During the years that he owned and operated the National Gas and Supply Company, a bottled gas appliance store at 7th and Jefferson, he was a good customer of

Petter Supply when I was employed there. He was an avid golfer and although we played in different foursomes, we would chat as we encountered one another on the course or in the clubhouse. Not one of the original Romeo's, he soon joined us and continued to meet regularly for the rest of his life. We were saddened when we learned of his death June 30,1994, from injuries sustained in an automobile accident at 31st and Jefferson. He was 77.

The Riekes were one of Paducah's pioneer families and prominent in the dry goods business. Jim was born in Paducah, July 3,1916, the son of James Calhoun and Helen Decker Rieke. He was a graduate of Tilghman High School and a 1938 graduate of Centre College, Danville, with a degree in business. He joined the staff of General Insurance Agency, and was treasurer until 1941. That year, he joined Lockheed-Vega Aircraft in Los Angeles. After Pearl Harbor, he enlisted in the U.S. Air Force, took pilot training, was commissioned a second lieutenant and flew more than 300 combat hours in the southwest Pacific fighting area. He was discharged in 1945 with the rank of captain. Jim founded the National Gas and Supply Company of Paducah and Marion, Kentucky, served as president, then sold the business in 1945 to Kengas, a subsidy of West Kentucky Gas. Between 1947 and 1957, he was general manager of the Paducah Bus Company, president of the Paducah Country Club, and director of Peoples Bank. In 1963, he became a director in Computer Services, Inc. a position he held until he retired in 1982. By 1965, he had become trust officer of Peoples Bank and was elected president in 1967. By the 1970s, he was named chairman of the board and chief operating officer. He was one of the founders of the Paducah McCracken Development Center, a Rotarian for 18 years, a past member of the Jaycees, and served a term as vice president of the Chamber of Commerce. He served on the Region Four Executive Committee of Boy Scouts, after having served as former district chairman, council treasurer, and council president of Boy Scouts Four River Council. In 1985 he was appointed acting city manager by the city board of commissioners.

He was married to Mary Deronda Stewart of Barboursville, Kentucky. They had four children: Mary Rieke Barker; James C.

Rieke, III (now deceased); William Rieke; and Louis Rieke. He was a lifelong member of the First Presbyterian Church and served for many years as elder and trustee.

JAMES L. HARDY

J im joined the Romeos soon after we began meeting. He was a senior partner in the law firm of Hardy, Terrell and Boswell. His firm constructed a new office at 426 South 6th Street, conveniently located near the McCracken County Court House.

He received his law degree from the University of Kentucky in 1950, and then started his practice in Paducah. He was a veteran of World War II and served in the U.S. Army Air Corps in Europe with the 305th Bomb Group for 38 months. He was married to Elizabeth Brown, and had one son, Michael Hardy, of Lexington, Kentucky, and daughters, Rebecca Holt, Charlotte, North Carolina, and Betty Jo Hendrickson, Paducah. He was a member of the First Presbyterian Church, the McCracken County Bar Association, the Kentucky Bar Association, and the American Bar Association. He died April 18,1993, age 75, and was buried in Mount Kenton Cemetery. Jim was a fun-loving guy, and enjoyed telling lawyer stories and jokes. He had a boyish zest for life and his sharp legal mind and serious demeanor masked his impish sense of humor.

JOHN W. HORNSBY

J ohn had been a city commissioner for a few years when he joined the Romeos. He moved to Paducah in 1953 from Fulton County, Kentucky, to work as a security analyst for Union Carbide, where he stayed until his retirement. He was a founding member of the Union Carbide Credit Union and served as president. He was a member of the Arcadia Methodist Church for 45 years, a member of the Paducah Masonic Lodge 449, and the American Legion. He served on the Paducah City Commission for 18 years and served on the Paducah Area Transit Board, the

Paducah-McCracken County Board for Senior Citizens and the Carson Park Board. He was a charter member of the Brooks Memorial Stadium Commission and a lifetime supporter of Paducah baseball. The most tragic event of his life was the loss of his son John Rogers Hornsby, who died in Vietnam in 1969. He was proud of his relationship to baseball legend Rogers Hornsby. John died September 2, 1999, and is survived by his wife of 51 years, Ava Nell Bennett Hornsby. He was buried in Woodlawn Memorial Gardens, Paducah.

Fellow Romeos, P.J. Grumley, and John, served on the city commission together for 10 years and worked closely with each other on many projects. He was a dear friend to all of us.

P. J. GRUMLEY

P.J Grumley was born to Paul E. and Esther (Dowers) Grumley on January 10, 1926 in Eugene, Vermillion County, Indiana. He was graduated from Newport, Indiana, High School May, 1943. He enlisted in the U.S. Navy January of 1944 and served as a hospital corpsman for 13 months in the South Pacific during World War II. After his discharge in 1946, he enrolled at Indiana College of Mortuary and graduated as an embalmer and funeral director. In August 1948, he married Mary Ruth Hussman. They have four children and eleven grandchildren. They moved to Paducah in August 1962 to go into business with his brother-in-law, H.L. Hussman.

They opened the first 15-cent hamburger restaurant in the area as Burger Chef. This business became very successful and grew to stores at three locations. In the early 1980s, P.J. retired and sold the stores to Hardee's. He joined the Lions Club in 1963, was chairman of the Lions Telethon in 1970, an annual event that raised substantial sums of money each year for charity, and served as Lions president in 1970-1971. He was chairman of the Retail Merchants Association in 1968, president of the Chamber of Commerce in 1971, and was involved with many committees, the Salvation Army,

Red Cross, and Boy Scouts.

He was elected to the Paducah City Commission in 1975, serving until 1980, then was reelected in 1984 and served a total of 19 years, with seven years as mayor pro tem, under mayors Murphy, Viterisi, Montgomery and Jones. They accomplished many changes and improvements during those years. P.J. learned to love Paducah and said it is the best place in the world to live.

I knew who P.J. was in his earlier years here, and ate at his restaurants occasionally. But it was when he moved on South Country Club Lane across from the Hanks, that I became personally acquainted with him. He joined our Friday lunch group and rarely missed a week. He would frequently phone me to be sure I was aware of our meeting place and would come by and pick me up if I didn't have other plans. I was always impressed by his hands-on way of handling his jobs as commissioner or when he was involved with other civic needs. I believe he spent 95 percent of his waking hours on civic matters, and I wondered how he had any time to relax and enjoy life. But he does enjoy being active and thrives on it. He is interested in baseball and attends many games at Brooks Stadium. He loves to fish and enjoys working in his garden and spending time with his children and grandchildren. And he continues today to keep busy and although retired, still concerns himself with public matters.

ELMER C. BREIDERT

Elmer C. Breidert's first meeting with our Friday lunch group was January 29, 1999, when he came as a guest of P.J. Grumley. He has been a regular ever since and has added another dimension to our get-togethers. He and P.J. usually come together and share a mutual interest in baseball at Brooks Park. Although I had not met Elmer previously, I was acquainted with who he was, for he has been visible around downtown, particularly during the summer festivals, when he was an active participant.

Elmer was born in St. Louis, Missouri, March 15,1927and attended grade and high schools there. While at Grover Cleveland

High School he was on the track and swimming teams. During his senior year, he won the Missouri state backstroke championship and was ranked 8th in the United States. In March 1945, with World War II still going on, Elmer, at age 17, still in high school, joined the Navy and served 18 months. He then went directly to college. He enrolled at the Missouri School of Mines and Metallurgy in Rolla and graduated in 1950 with a degree in chemical engineering. While in college, he continued his swimming career.

He married his high school sweetheart, Dorothy, in 1947 and they had their first child shortly after his graduation. He worked for Carter Carburetor in St. Louis for two years, for the Air Force one year, then moved his family to Paducah in 1953 to work as a chemical engineer for Union Carbide Nuclear Company. He retired in 1983 with 30 years of continuous service. This was precipitated by a massive brain hemorrhage, which severely restricted his ability to work.

He started the first Paducah Swim Team around 1962 and was strictly a volunteer coach, while Dorothy and other parents did the necessary work. He was also a volunteer for the American Red Cross for over twenty years and taught hundreds of children and adults for free. Dorothy and all six of their children taught in the Red Cross "Learn to Swim" program for many years. When Tom Wilson was mayor of Paducah in 1963, he asked Elmer to be in charge of the river activities during the summer festival, including the cross-river swim. Elmer was not only in charge of that part of the festival, but swam in the river cross for many years, as did his children. Floodwall artist Robert Dafford, painted a mural in the spring of 2001 depicting the festival, which included a painting of Elmer and his six children: Stephanie, Janice, Tom, Chuck, Mike and Teresa, emerging from the river after their swim. The Breiderts paid the cost of the mural, which also includes hot-air balloons, parachutists, children at a watermelon grab, and the Paducah Symphony. Elmer and Dorothy are retired and live on Afton Avenue. They have 18 grandchildren and 5 great-grandchildren.

BARRON WHITE

He was born March 1914 in Memphis, Tennessee, and moved to Paducah in 1923. He attended Lee Elementary, Jefferson, Washington Junior High and Tilghman High schools, graduating in 1931. He worked in his father's grocery until his father died in May 1933. In August 1933 he went to work for Petter Supply, in the shipping department.

White was drafted into the Army Air Force in 1942 and graduated from Officers Candidate School and commissioned a second lieutenant in August 1943. He served with the First Air Defense Command in Philadelphia and Norfolk and was sent to England in March 1944 with the 303rd Fighter Wing, where he attended Royal Air Force Controller School and trained with the Royal Navy on an LST in the North Sea. After D-Day, he was flown to France and served with the XXIX Tactical Command, Ninth Air Force in Belgium, Holland and Germany. After Germany surrendered, he was one of a group of forty who were flown to San Diego, California, and assigned with the U.S. Navy, headed for Japan. But the war ended and all were permitted to leave the service. He resigned his commission with the rank of captain.

He resumed work with Petter Supply, traveled four states for three years, and then was brought into the office to head a department. In 1989 he retired at age 75.

In 1957, Barron married Zelma Nicholson of Reidland. The Whites have two daughters, Kathy, now a professional musician, who performs with a quintet and plays with symphonies in Atlanta and several surrounding states; and Liz, married to Joe Hansen, a Methodist minister and father of three teenagers, in Waynesville, Ohio. Barron has been active in the Boy Scouts, Jaycees, Rotary Club, and has served several terms on the Advisory Board of the Associated General Contractors of West Kentucky. Since retirement, he has enjoyed doing volunteer work for a number of organizations, including the Paducah Ambassadors, the floodwall mural committee, the veterans parade committee, the area Purple Heart chapter, the Friends of the McCracken County Library Board, and the PCC Seniors Board. Other interests have included swimming, flying, photography, writing and golf.

HERMAN EUGENE KATTERJOHN JR

Herman Eugene "Gene" Katterjohn began meeting with the Romeos a short time after the first get-together and has continued to do so, when available. Since he is not fully retired and still serves on a number of boards, he has to miss many meetings with the lunch group, but when is able to do so, he will phone and offer to furnish transportation.

Gene was born May 4, 1921, the son of Herman and Lucille Shelton Katterjohn, at the family home on South Eleventh Street. His grandfather and great-grandfather lived next door, and other family members lived in the area. Gene is the sixth generation Katterjohn to live in "Germantown," as the neighborhood was listed in the mid-1800s. The Katterjohn Brick Company, established in 1871, was located behind the row of Katterjohn homes on Eleventh Street near the former Illinois Central Railroad Depot. Clay for the brick company was mined from the banks of Island Creek, which meandered for several miles inland from its mouth south of Broad Street to 1-24 near Husband Road.

As a young man, Gene remembers tramping through the densely wooded bottoms of Island Creek, less than a block from his home. He attended St. Mary's Academy through the fifth grade, finished the sixth at Longfellow and went to Washington Junior High. He finished the ninth and tenth grades at Tilghman High then, as he wanted to attend West Point or Annapolis, he enrolled at Columbia Military School. But after finishing the twelfth grade he took the physical exam for both academies and found he was too near-sighted to pass. So after consulting with his father, he decided to attend pharmacy school at Purdue University, which was one of the finest in the country.

He was in his first semester of his sophomore year at Purdue when Japan bombed Pearl Harbor. Like all other schools, Purdue changed its education system to adjust to wartime conditions. When Gene returned to school after the Christmas break, he learned he could continue his education until graduation if he maintained at least a C-plus average and attended classes six days a week. Otherwise, he would be drafted. Since Purdue was a land grant school, there was a requirement that all physically able boys were to take two years of military ROTC training, with those making high grades being able to continue with their military training through the junior and senior years. Those graduating in senior ROTC would receive second lieutenant commissions in the Army reserve. After completing a semester of junior military, he was accepted in the senior ROTC artillery program. His next two years were difficult because in addition to his pharmacy studies he had to master the requirements to be a field artillery officer. Although he had completed the requirements to become a registered pharmacist, he still needed to pass the state test. The state board decided that he could take the test in February before graduating in August. He completed the two years of military ROTC and graduated in August 1943. (He passed the state test and his Kentucky pharmacy diploma was issued in Frankfort February 1944, a year after he was on active duty). The morning after graduation, all military graduates left in a convoy of eight trucks to Fort Benjamin Harrison, Indiana, where they were given physicals and issued clothing. All received orders to attend artillery officer's training school at Fort Sill, Oklahoma.

Gene said the OCS course was physically and mentally tough, but he finished in the top 25 percent of the class. He was sent to Fort Bragg, North Carolina, to train in a "Long Tom" heavy artillery battery. After 60 days, he was activated to the 744th Field Artillery Battalion, a part of a division of 144 eight-inch howitzers stationed at Camp Chaffee, Arkansas. It was a fine unit, composed from an Eastern National Guard Coastal Artillery unit from New Jersey. He "loved the 744th because it was well trained with excellent officers, but I was left behind with 25 other excess officers when the entire division moved to Europe. After this, I was transferred to a 105mm howitzer unit, which did not thrill me." After a few months with the 105th howitzer unit, he volunteered to be a liaison pilot for the artillery. He passed the flight physical and asked to be relieved from duty with the 105th, but was turned down twice by his commanding officer, who did not want the problem of training a new officer. About this time, the German army was making a push against the Americans and the British in the battle which became known as the Battle of the Bulge. The U.S. lost a large number of liaison pilots in the battle and all who had applied were called on an emergency basis to report to the air base at Sheppard Field, Texas. He completed his basic flight training, two months of short field landings and take-offs, also intensive training in control of the L-4 Piper aircraft, as well as instrument training in a Stearman. Before graduation, he was asked to serve as instructor and remained to train three classes. He was then promoted to be an operations pilot, making special flights to Army and Navy bases in Texas and Oklahoma.

He was released from active duty April 14,1946 and returned to Paducah to live with his parents at 1106 Caldwell, next to their drugstore. He worked for his dad as a registered pharmacist for 9 months, and then was offered a job as pharmacist for Clarence Bennett at the Gilbert-Bennett drugstore at 6th and Broadway. After working there for nine months, he was offered a job by Abbott Laboratories as a professional service representative to cover 28 counties in Kentucky and four in Tennessee. He spent almost four years calling on doctors, dentists, hospitals, drugstores, and veterinarians, plus the two wholesale houses in Paducah. Gene says he loved the work and did better financially than he could have had he stayed in retail pharmacy. But after he and Carolyn Owen married and Susan was born, being away from home three and four nights a week was not conducive to being a family man. He decided to see if his father-in-law, Horace Owen, was still interested in his coming into the business with him at Owen Cleaners. The answer was yes, and they worked out a partnership agreement, which lasted for 22 years, after which they formed a corporation. Gene says his total time as a partner and major stockholder was forty-two years. Three years after he joined Owen Cleaners, he was called back to active duty during the Korean War. He reported back to Fort Sill, Oklahoma, where he resumed being a flight instructor in Army aviation, flying L-4s, L-5s, L-14s and L- 22 aircraft. During the last six months of his 18-month tour, he was assigned to the 7th Division, Army Aviation Section, stationed south of the Chorwan Reservoir. From this airfield, he performed aerial observation, directing fire of artillery and air strikes..

Upon finishing his service in Korea, he returned to Paducah and resumed operating Owen Cleaners. The company business grew from one location at Tenth and Broadway to eight stores at strategic locations all over town. They received many honors during the 42 years - the most gratifying being invited to join Varsity International, the outstanding dry cleaners of the world. For fourteen years, Gene attended their annual meetings, and then declined in later years to concentrate on his directorship of the Paducah Bank and Trust Company, where he has served as director since 1957, and was chairman of the board for fourteen years. In 1991, he sold Owen Cleaners to his daughter, Carolyn, and her husband David Perry, retaining ownership of the real estate. Gene says he has recovered from the tragedy of losing his wife Carolyn in 1989 and is "fortunate to have married Mary Louise Ezell, who lost her husband two years prior to my losing Carolyn."

Gene commented, "From now on, I'm enjoying life, traveling, and seeing Owen Cleaners thrive under the leadership of Carolyn and David."

RECOLLECTIONS OF THE WAR YEARS

CAREER INTERRUPTED

What turned into a 50-plus-year employment at Petter Supply Company was put on temporary hiatus when I received "Greetings" from the government in March, 1942. After induction into the Army in October that year with two others from Paducah, George "Brownie" Wedel and Tom "Buck" Willingham, I was sent to Jefferson Barracks in St. Louis, Missouri, for 16 weeks of basic training. Buck received a medical discharge midway through basic, Brownie was sent to radio school, and my orders sent me to Parks Air College in East St. Louis to an engine mechanic's school. Although I made the highest grades at the school and was selected to be the acting school sergeant, I did not want to be a mechanic, knowing that a pilot's life might be dependent on my ability to keep a plane flight-worthy. I had never been mechanically proficient and knew my limitations. I had applied for officer candidate school on my 90th day of service (a requirement to apply) and hoped to get a new assignment. Before this came through, our entire graduating class was shipped to Brookley Field, Mobile, Alabama, and placed into a repair squadron for actual training work on B-24 and B-17 engines. My application papers to OCS followed me to Mobile and within a few weeks, my orders came through to report to the Air Force Officers' Candidate School in Miami Beach, Florida.

After completing the 90-day course, I was classified as a supply officer, but before this was put through, a number of us with flying experience were reclassified to be flight controllers. At the same

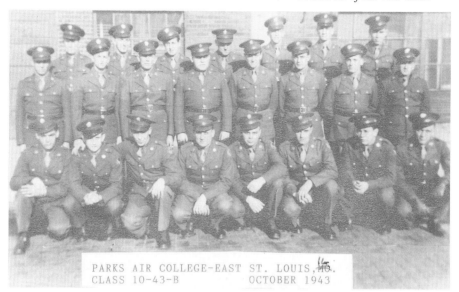

PARKS AIR COLLEGE-EAST ST. LOUIS, MO.
CLASS 10-43-B   OCTOBER 1943

1943-Parks Air College-East St. Louis, Missouri; Barron White, Second from Right,
Second Row

time, the "Glider Guider" program was phased out and those men were also reclassified. So I joined a group of about fifty new second lieutenants and was sent to the Air Force School of Applied Tactics in Orlando, Florida. We were to learn how to use radar. It had just become a useful tool for the Air Force and we were among the first to be trained as fighter control officers. The official job description of our duties was, "To direct interception of enemy air raids reported directly or through an air warning system; to instruct friendly fighter planes to place, time and altitude to meet the attacking aircraft; to determine whether anti-aircraft defenses were to handle partial or total defenses; to keep friendly airplanes informed on location, speed direction and altitude and to assist them in returning to their own or friendly bases after missions; to supervise operation of a central area control room; must be familiar with types, speeds and capabilities of friendly fighter aircraft and enemy bombardment planes; to be able to evaluate relative strengths of enemy air attacks and to determine the number and type of aircraft to successfully meet them; to be skilled in the use and operation of radar information. Officers must be selected for this responsible work on the basis of alertness,

Lt. Egbert Barron White-
1943

quick thinking and
capacity to make accu-
rate decisions based on
quickly observed data."

We took a course
in aircraft recognition,
were taught how to
interpret "blips" on a
radar screen and to
determine height, speed
and direction of all air-
craft by connecting the
moving images that
appeared on the scope.
At the completion of this
course in October, most
of us were sent to the
First Air Force, Mitchel Field, New York. Harvey White of
Richmond, Virginia, and Ed Yawney of Long Island, New York,
and I traveled together to our new post. We were interviewed, then
assigned to the 93rd Fighter Control Squadron, Bradley Field,
Connecticut, where we went through several weeks of working
with several squadrons of fighter pilots as they flew their missions
up and down the coast. Around mid-November we were sent to
the Philadelphia wing of the First Air Force, which was charged
with the air defense of the Atlantic Coast between New York and
Norfolk, Virginia.

Our control section had supervision over cities, airports,
searchlights, anti-craft artillery and all military installations.
Controllers were trained to act quickly to all conditions, to make
accurate assessments of situations that arose and to react accord-
ingly. We were under the direction of Chief Controller, Major

Freshman Orientation, Officers Candidate School, Miami, Florida-1943

John Glenn of Martha's Vineyard. Our operation occupied most of the sixth floor of the Lincoln-Liberty building in downtown Philadelphia. We controllers sat in a glass-enclosed booth overlooking a large plot board, on which had been painted a map of the East Coast. Around the four sides of the board sat a group of enlisted men with headphones, which were connected to spotters and satellite radar sites at all points of the area. As they received information on planes flying they marked the location of each on the board with a "Christmas tree" to indicate plane type, number of planes and direction. Controllers could see the entire air traffic by looking at the board, so with radio contact to all military aircraft, they could take any necessary action. There were 16 controllers working eight-hour shifts round the clock. We would take turns at night being chief controller, the period between midnight until 6 a.m. being the time of least air activity.

There was one regularly scheduled flight daily, a Pan Am Clipper flying boat that took off from Bermuda to the East Coast at 3 every morning. It was supposed to turn on its responder so it could be challenged by our radar to confirm it was friendly. We were warned to check this flight, and if we did not get a response, we were to call our airfield to "scramble" the pair of pilots in their planes at the end of the runway with engines running; ready to go up and visually determine their identity. Many mornings the Clipper failed to identify itself until the last minute and this gave we novice controllers a few anxious moments. We had been told that the enemy could shoot down the plane and fly in its place, so we had to be alert to this possibility. After a few weeks we got rid of the anxious feeling of responsibility and felt more confident of our ability to be controllers.

Working eight-hours on and 16 hours off began to seem like a day at the office. Instead of living in a bachelor officer's quarters, we shared rooms on the second floor of the Sylvania Hotel, within a block and a half of work. When we had rain or snow, we took the elevator to the hotel basement and walked the subway to the basement of the Lincoln-Liberty building and then took the elevator to the control room.

As 1943 came to a close, we received orders to proceed to Norfolk to report to the control room upstairs over the post office. I took the train and arrived in Norfolk the night before Christmas. Other controllers, most of whom lived nearby, took the transfer time to visit their families, but as my home was in Kentucky, I did not have this option. So I woke up Christmas morning to an empty barracks and spent Christmas Day alone, and walked across the street for a bite to eat at noon. We were stationed in Norfolk for over a month until our orders came for us to be moved overseas to Europe.

FROM NORFOLK TO NEW YORK
February to March 1944

When we left Norfolk, we assumed we would sail for England within the week, but we were sent to a staging area and were there from February until the first of March. We were given an APO c/o New York address even though we were still in the States. I have not determined exactly where we were, but know that it was about a half hour's drive from New York City. One particular incident that happened while there comes to mind. One of our new lieutenants, Julius Bloom, could spend the nights with his parents, as they lived in Brooklyn, New York. He went shopping one afternoon and came back to the barracks wearing cowboy boots, a western jacket and a "ten-gallon" cowboy hat. It did not seem to bother him when we kidded him and called him, a "cowboy from Brooklyn." But he apparently left it at home, for he did not wear the outfit again.

Three days before we sailed a shipping notice was posted on the bulletin board indicating that we were now on "Ship Alert Status" and that we were confined to quarters to await orders to sail on the *Queen Mary* from New York City for England. As everyone emerged from the mess hall and began to read the notice and walk away, Julius read it several times, then his face turned white, then he fainted and fell to the floor. He was sent to the post infirmary and that was the last time we saw him. He did not sail with us and I do not know if he was sent over later with another unit. Several said that he suffered from "gang-plank" knees.

When we learned that we would be leaving for England and would be sailing on the *Queen Mary*, many of us had mixed emotions. Anxiety was accompanied with excitement, and eagerness to get going. The papers were filled with war headlines and stories of ship sinkings. There were stories about how the British had set up a convoy system for merchant ships from Halifax in Canada to the British Isles, with air patrols to protect them by covering much of the route. We read that the German U-boats constantly menaced

Allied shipping. There had been articles about the Germans having developed "wolf packs," teams of from 2 to 20 submarines operating together to attack convoys in the North Atlantic. In March 1943, the Allied High Command had given the British and Canadian Navy the primary job of protecting North American convoys. As the *Queen Mary* was British owned, we felt that we would be protected. We were informed that the ship had a cruising speed of 28 knots, giving it a significant edge in speed over escorts or submarines; therefore it would make the journey without escorts.

A DATE WITH THE "QUEEN"

An Army truck collected our bedrolls and took off for the New York docks. Inside my roll I had put my small radio with a hope that it would arrive intact. Several other trucks picked us up, each of us loaded down with a large canvas duffel bag and B-4 suit bag that contained our belongings. We assembled at dockside and proceeded up the gangplank into the hold of the *Queen Mary*, now painted a dull gray. We were directed to our quarters and given ID tags, which designated deck and bunk numbers. Our tag color matched a painted stripe on our deck. All aboard were required to stay in the area that matched their deck color. It took several hours to get all the many groups aboard.

Although the ship had been designed for 2,000 passengers and a crew of 920, it had been converted for wartime use with 5,500 berths. After the "Queen" was assigned to the Atlantic Ocean to ferry American troops to the European front, additional berths and hammocks were added to hold over 15,000 troops. There were hammocks swung on the "tween" decks, even in the bow and stern sections. Our room had six bunks, which left space only for getting in and out.

Finally we were pushed away from shore by tugboats and with a number of blasts from the ship's three steam whistles, headed for the Atlantic Ocean. As we sailed by the Statue of Liberty we gave

Leaving for Europe, Going Away Party, Navy Officer Club, Norfolk, Virginia

it a last long look and wondered if we would make it back. In a few hours we cleared the last bit of land and settled in for the week-long voyage. Several second lieutenants in our group were assigned to be deck traffic officers. We were assigned a spot amidship, at the head of the companionway on each deck to expedite the movement of enlisted men who came from the port and starboard sides of the outer corridors down the steps to the mess hall. At mealtime, it sounded and looked like roundup time at the old corral, with tin mess kits clanging and hanging from their belts. When the meal was over, the men were hurried up the steps so the next group could eat. The mess hall for all enlisted men was located amidship several decks below the Promenade deck.

Officers ate in the main dining room. This was originally the dining room on "C" deck for first class passengers and the ceiling was three decks high the entire width of the ship. Many men became seasick after eating, and some did not get over their nausea for the entire trip. Several times while on duty this feeling hit me after seeing others in distress. It helped me to get over mine by eating very little or not at all for several meals. Those who had the most difficulty were the men in hammocks in the bow. They were subjected to more of the pitch and rolling motion than those of us in the middle.

In a day or so we became accustomed to the ship motion and to our daily routine. For the most part the weather was pleasant and it was fun to go out to the poop deck and see the long white zigzag wake as we moved thru the water. The pilot changed directions a few degrees every minute. We sailed alone, without escort as the ship's speed of over 28 knots was said to keep us safe from submarine attack. When we got about halfway across, the higher waves caused more ship motion and we would go to the dining hall and stretch out on the deck and listen to music. I don't remember having movies, but there must have been some elsewhere on shipboard. On March 9 we arrived in Scotland after a safe and pleasant trip.

EUROPEAN THEATER OF OPERATIONS

MARCH 1943-AUGUST 1945

After becoming the 303rd Fighter Control Squadron, we left the United States March 1943, boarded the *Queen Mary* from New York and sailed to England. We steamed thru the Firth of Clyde and dropped anchor in the Firth of Forth, in the middle of a group of naval vessels, including a few baby flat-top carriers, on a gray, overcast and foggy morning. We landed at Greenoch, Scotland, and then had a day's train ride from Glasgow through central England, through London to Ashford, Kent, south of London and a few miles inland from the English Channel.

After a cold two weeks in tents, we controllers, Capt. Oscar Schafer, from New York City; 1st Lieut. Tom Reis, from Evansville, Indiana; and second lieutenants Howard Sharpe, from Charleston, South Carolina; Don Baldwin, from Myrtle Beach, South Carolina; and this boy from Paducah, Kentucky; were sent to Stanmore, north of London, to attend a Royal Air Force controller school. We trained with the British controllers for a month, and then were sent 200 miles north of London to a Royal Navy fighter director tender, docked at Hull, on the east coast. This ship, an LST, was loaded with 40 tons of lead on the deck to minimize pitch and roll, and had been converted into a radar control station. We shared 4-hour watches with British controllers, while doing patrol duty in the North Sea about 15 miles off the coast. Twice while on watch we were looked over by German reconnaissance planes, but no shots were exchanged. Once during our tour, the deck officer throttled back to idle so they could swap cigarettes for a basket of fish from a small boat trawling nearby. Oddly, the captain, a big ruddy-faced Irishman with a red beard, became seasick as soon as we left the dock and stayed in his bunk for the entire voyage.

We landed at Grimsby and took a train back to our 303rd group, which had moved to Biggin Hill, a Royal Air Force airdrome a mile east of the town of Bromley, Kent. We would be billeted there for several months, until after D-Day. One of my first needs after returning was to get my hair cut, so I hitched a jeep ride to town to a little one-chair shop that catered to U.S. servicemen. There was a soldier ahead of me, so I sat in a chair beside a coat rack that had a mirror behind it facing the chair. The soldier had hung his carbine on the rack by its strap. When he got out of the chair and reached over for his weapon, he dropped it and it discharged, shattering the mirror, not too many inches from where I was sitting. Needless to say, I was shaken. I still remember the date, as it happened March 24, on my birthday. I left there and walked down the street to a Christian Science reading room to settle my nerves a little. A nice lady attendant, after a nice little chat, told me she worked for a family that liked to have servicemen as their guests, so invited me to tea and dinner the following week.

I arrived at the address given me, which was out in the countryside, with a long winding tree-lined drive back to an old stone house. I met a lady in the front garden watering her flowers. She told me she was using her bath water, which they always saved due to wartime conservation. She introduced herself as Lady Mildred Fitzgerald, owner of the estate, which she said had been in the family for over a century. She escorted me upstairs to a guest room, with

Royal Air Force Control Center, "The Rookery", Biggin Hill, England

instructions to meet her other guests in the parlor for tea at four o'clock. At tea, she introduced me to her husband, Sir Gerald Fitzgerald, who was retired and resplendent in his British uniform with its row of medals. Among the guests were several other British servicemen. I was the only American. After tea and a typical British meal, we went to an adjoining room for drinks and sweets. Lady

Mildred told us of the war work they did and of the many people from other countries who have stayed with them, including a few prominent dignitaries. It was obvious that they loved to entertain, especially service people. Colonel Fitzgerald told us he loved American music, particularly our jazz, of which he had acquired a large collection. He played a number of records and went over to his set of drums and beat out the tempo with the music. It was a very nice evening away from the usual routine.

Biggin Hill was an airdrome surrounded by a battery of barrage balloons, tethered by wire cables and raised several hundred feet to prevent low-flying aircraft from penetrating the air space. Several anti-aircraft batteries were situated at intervals around the area. The headquarters was in a two-story brick building that contained a mess hall, a bar, officers' clubrooms and sleeping quarters for the higher-ranking officers. The rest of us were billeted in cottages on the outskirts of the field. In addition to our 30 officers, there were British, Canadian, Scottish, Polish, and Australian officers from many air force units. All men ate in the mess hall in the headquarters building. It appeared to have been a country club at one time.

Every day, we were transported to our operations, about a mile down the hill toward Bromley. The building was surrounded by a high wall and had a single entrance gate, where a guard was stationed day and night. Inside were several levels of glass-enclosed control positions overlooking a large operations room with a large grid-marked plot board around which was seated enlisted British Women's Auxiliary Air Force personnel (WAAFS) with headphones. On the board was painted a map of England marked off with coded areas. The two lower levels were for the British, we Americans had the third level and the fourth level was for the other Allied personnel, including Chinese, Polish, and Norwegians. This was "The Rookery," the fighter control nerve center of British and American operations for the United States and Royal air forces.

There were three-eight-hour shifts assigned to all sixteen officers in our controller's section, which we worked seven days a week until several weeks after D-Day. Then landing strips were constructed in Normandy for all Allied Air Force planes. Until that time, our American fighter planes continued to fly combat missions from British bases at Ashford, Kingsnorth, and Woodchurch, on the coast near the channel.

Since company grade officers did not rate being furnished with transportation, we took advantage of using a number of bicycles available at the airfield. This enabled us to see some of the surrounding countryside when we had time off. We discovered a riding stable nearby and several of us rented horses when our afternoons were free. Our usual breakfast at the mess hall was either powdered eggs, baked beans on toast, kippered herring, or a brown mush that looked and tasted like cream of wheat. We discovered a French couple who lived about a mile down the road on the coast, where we could get a breakfast for about five shillings. We went there about once a week to enjoy their fresh eggs, milk, and ripe tomatoes - a refreshing change from the British meals that were not very tasty. The family told us that they had relatives who lived across the channel near the French coast and made an occasional crossing to smuggle in fresh farm products.

On another one of our bicycle journeys around the area we located a little pub that offered apple cider that they aged in old whiskey barrels. After a cold mug or two, the trip home was sometimes a challenge with Army vehicles traveling up and down the road severely testing our steering abilities.

I missed my little radio that I had rolled up in my bedroll before shipping overseas. Shortly after we landed, our control section left Ashford for school, saw duty at sea, and then was sent to Biggin Hill, while the rest of the 303rd Wing was training at Ashford. I had phoned the supply sergeant at Ashford several times to ask if my roll had arrived and was told it had not. So one afternoon after getting off duty, Jimmie Keen, Dick Hazlewood and I borrowed a jeep and drove down to Ashford for a visit, our first since landing over two months ago. I went to the supply room and asked if my bedroll and radio had come. The sergeant said it had not. Just then I saw a little radio on a shelf behind the sergeant. It was my radio and had my name and Army serial number on the back. They had been using it for over a month. So I got it and took it back with me to Biggin Hill.

But my problem was not over. When I got back to my billet, without thinking, I plugged it into a receptacle and blew out all of the tubes. I forgot that the outlets there were 220-volt and my radio was 110. I made a list of the seven tubes and at the first opportunity, caught a train to London to search for replacements. I found all but the power tube after visiting several shops at Piccadilly Circus, but that last tube took me several more trips until it was located. Then with the addition of a transformer, I was finally back in business. It helped me pass away many long lonely hours during my off-duty hours.

When I wrote the story (In England-1943) I devoted only eight lines to our month's schooling at Stanmore. Then in July 2001, my good friend Ed Hank loaned me a book entitled, "The Ultra Secret," (F.W. Winterbottom, 1974) which revealed the first account of the "most astounding cryptanalysis of World War II, - how the British broke the German code and read most of signals between Hitler and his generals throughout the war."

Several weeks after we landed in England in March 1943, we were sent to Stanmore, a British Royal Air Force school a few miles north of London for further training to be fighter control officers. Stanmore was the second train stop from London. We were there a month working under simulated flight conditions. The main building and a few smaller buildings had been a family estate with surrounding grounds that occupied a city block. Tall trees and shrubbery encircled the area with a single vehicular drive and gate, nestled among a row of private homes. We were billeted with local people, two to a home. Most of the families we met worked in London. They would bring us a pot of hot tea to our room, serve us breakfast, and then walk around the corner to catch the shuttle train to the city. Little did they know then that Stanmore was the Supreme Fighter Command Headquarters for the entire Allied operation. While our training exercises occupied the entire ground floor, the command center was way below in a deep underground operations room where Air Marshall "Stuffy" Dowding was the director of intelligence. It was there that the captured German cipher machine ENIGMA (after refinements, renamed ULTRA) was housed, the machine that enabled the Allies to crack enemy coded messages, which they used throughout the war. Churchill, Eisenhower and many of the commanders at the highest level were privy to this information, but this was tightly secured and all of the American and British officers that were at Stanmore were totally unaware of this information. There was an official ban on any reference to ULTRA until the spring of 1974.

MAY 1944, OUR FINAL MONTH BEFORE D-DAY

As the time before the invasion narrowed to the final few weeks, we were kept very busy at operations. Our four squadrons of P-47s were flying missions every day the weather would permit. Even when the weather was bad, our pilots were kept on the ready and every controller position was manned full time around the clock. Channel "C," the air-sea-rescue position, saw the most action, for with all the flying activity, there was a steady stream of calls for help and information. Although radio discipline was ordered, there were many times when you would hear radio conversations about the awesome spectacles fliers were witnessing as they flew their missions. The enormous mass of vehicles, tanks, ships, and vessels assembled on the shores and water up and down the coast was a spectacle to behold. Although we knew D-Day was imminent, we who had worked the June 5 day shift were surprised when we reported for duty the next morning to learn that the invasion had started just after midnight. All squadrons flew continuous missions from daylight to dusk. All we did was work, eat, and sleep and back to work, for the next few weeks.

Shortly after D-Day, the Germans began to send over their V-1 "Buzz" bombs. They had launching positions in France, Belgium, and Germany, all pointed toward London. Three or four times a day, they would send these pilotless aircraft to England, usually at breakfast, noon and dinner time - times they considered would be most disruptive. Bombs would be launched from several positions simultaneously for maximum effect. Many days we could see as many as three overhead at the same time, each from a different direction, headed for London. They flew at a constant altitude, and at a constant speed, with just enough fuel to reach their destinations. A number of these were snagged by the barrage balloons and cables. British and American pilots also knocked down a number before they hit their targets in the heavily populated areas. The blast of the 2,000-pound bombs when they exploded had a devastating effect on Londoners. Later records indicated that over 1,000 of these unmanned killers rained on London and environs during the month of June. Large sections of the city were demolished during the period.

City dwellers took to the bomb shelters whenever the air raid alarm sounded. Thousands spent nights in the underground subways. Then early one morning one of the bombs hit a balloon cable over our area. This shut off the engine and caused the plane to dive silently to the ground. It hit right outside our billet and exploded, creating a hole 30 feet in diameter and 15 feet deep. It completely obliterated a British staff car parked next to the building and caused almost half of our building to collapse. The horizontal blast was felt for several blocks, with all windows within that area blown out. We had just eaten breakfast and had come back to our rooms. I had finished my shower and had put on a pair of shorts when the bomb went off outside our window. The blast knocked me from the bathroom into the bedroom and partially under a table against the wall. A shower of glass, bricks and debris covered me. The room was filled with smoke and dust. For a moment I was too stunned to think or move. But as I heard others in the building clambering outside, I crawled out from under and headed for the nearest door. We gathered near the crater and took inventory. We were all covered with black dust and looked like coal miners. Fortunately, no one was killed and Capt. Dick Hazlewood of Ft. Worth, Texas, and I were the only ones wounded with minor cuts and bruises. Lt. Jimmie Kean of Brooklyn, New York, had been asleep upstairs and said he had a hard time getting out of bed because of the load of bricks.

Over half of the building was in shambles and we were soon moved to new quarters. We were grateful to have come out with our lives. We continued to endure the daily onslaught of the flying bombs, but since our new quarters had a large basement, we bedded down there for the rest of our stay in England and were able to get our sleep and rest.

It was not until August that our airstrips could be built on Normandy, so our air squadrons continued to fly daily missions from bases in England. Then as soon as we could be sent to France, we flew over. We were happy to get away from the buzz bombs and ready to face new challenges.

WITH THE NINTH AIR FORCE IN FRANCE

As soon as the airstrips were ready in France, our 303rd Air Wing flew over to Normandy and set up operations in Carentan, near St. Mere Eglese. We became the headquarters for the XIX Tactical Air Command, with nine fighter groups, one with P-51 and eight with P-47 aircraft. There were three from our 303rd wing, four from the 100th, one from the 70th, and one from the 84th wing. Company grade officers, captain and lower, were put in a row of canvas tents behind a chateau that had been the headquarters for German officers. Our field grade officers, major and higher rank, were housed in the chateau, which also contained the mess hall for all headquarters personnel.

By the end of August the radio news reported the fall of Paris to the Allies. Since the battle line was now on the east side of Paris, except for our daily duties at the control center working with our pilots as they flew their missions, it was peaceful and quiet back at the chateau. Every morning before breakfast, we saw a French woman tend to her one cow that she kept tethered to a stake in a small rectangular plot. The cow ate all the grass in a circle, then the next day was moved to the next area. After each move the woman

XIX TAC Barracks for Duty Officers; Captain Rank and Below-in tents; Major Rank and Higher-in chateau-Fall-1944-St. Mere Eglise, France

raked the dried manure over the cropped area, so the grass would grow back. It took her about two weeks to get back to the starting point.

The entire area was rural and many of the homes had dirt floors and people housed their livestock in a room in the house. We made visits into St. Mere Eglese, where most of the houses were clustered around the town' s Catholic church. We took a jeep one day to Cherbourg, where a lot of construction was underway to repair the seaport. We encountered several friends in other nearby units. We visited with Harry J. Livingston and Louis Fisher, two Paducahans, and with Harvey White, a roommate at OCS, who was with the IXTAC. We visited a company of Army nurses who had come over on the *Queen Mary* with us. They were encamped nearby, living in tents, wore GI clothing, helmets, leggings and combat boots, like our troops.

In September we moved south about a 100 kilometers to Rennes, near the Brest peninsular. While there we heard that Lieutenant General Patton had arrived and would take over the

Mont St. Michel, Brest Peninsula, France

Third Army and that our IXTAC would support him. Patton had "liberated" a cave full of wines and other liquors and issued an order that every soldier in his command receive an equal portion. It amounted to seven bottles each.

About once a week Colonel James McGehee, commander of the 406th Fighter Group took me along as he did a weather reconnaissance flight over the Atlantic. We would fly for an hour eastward and radio back to headquarters the information, including cloud cover at various altitudes, and general conditions. This information was vital to weather control, since the weather always moved west to east. Pilots flying back from missions could be told what weather to expect at home base. Col. McGehee, who had been transferred to headquarters after completing 50 missions with the group, enjoyed these trips away from combat. He always got on the group frequency on his return flights and if another pilot was in the area, they would get together and have a dog fight. On several missions, we flew up and down the coastline for these "exercises" and several times we "buzzed" Mont St. Michel, a prominent landmark on an island off the Brest peninsular. On one occasion, he flew between the islands of Jersey and Guernsey, 10 miles off the west coast of the Normandy peninsular, just to aggravate the Germans who continued to occupy the islands throughout the war. Each one had one 88-millimeter cannon battery and as we flew by, they shot off several rounds at us. Col. McGehee flew just high enough and away from the range of their guns to avoid getting hit. Each time a black puff of flak would burst near us, Col. McGehee would turn around, with half a cigar clinched between his teeth, grin, and ask me if that was close enough. I'd say, "Too close." Every burst scared the hell out of me, but I tried not to show it.

WITH THE NINTH AIR FORCE IN FRANCE AND BELGIUM

While we were operating in Normandy, Lt. Olen Waters of Clovis, New Mexico, a pilot assigned to headquarters, invited me to fly with him on several pick-up trips. On one occasion, while returning to our base, Lt. Waters said we were low on fuel and that we should stop at the nearest field for gas. We flew into a base in the British sector in the vicinity of Bayeux, west of Caen. A corporal said their petrol was limited and he had no authority to supply us. We asked him to have his CO call our base, which he agreed to do, but told us that it was tea time and we would have to wait. So we walked over to the officer's club to wait. The "club" was a large rectangular tent with a bar and tables with white cloths, and chairs. Even though a tough fight was going on near there, as the British were trying to break out of the Caen area, they were not about to give up their perks and tea time. After a short wait, the "O.K." call came through and we were able fly back to our post.

We were at Rennes for a very short time. Then, orders came through that we were moving to St. Quentin, about 125 kilometers northwest of Paris, near the Dutch-Belgium border. The wing packed up and moved by truck caravan to the new post. Several officers flew the headquarters aircraft. Lt. Waters and I flew in one of them. I don't recall the model, but it was a two-seater similar to the BT-13 Air Force trainer. We flew northwest until we crossed the Seine, then turned south towards Paris. As we approached the city, it became cloudy and smoky. We could hardly make out the Eiffel Tower until we were almost there. Lt. Waters called back to me that he was going to land there, as he needed to have the rudder control wiring checked. Although I suspected that it was a ruse to stop in Paris, I was all for it and did not object. We set down at Villacoublay Airfield, which was about 28 kilometers southeast of Paris and slightly south of Orley Field, and signed in. He had an American mechanic look over the problem. The mechanic said it could take a while to get to it and make repairs. So we decided to spend the night and caught a ride into Paris.

We checked into a midtown hotel for American soldiers, and then walked down the street until we spotted a restaurant where we had a good meal. The next morning we went back to the airport and waited until the plane was ready. We took off for St. Quentin and were there by noon. Colonel McGehee was not at all happy with us, said he feared something had happened to us, and threatened to slap AWOL charges against us, saying we just wanted to see Paris. But after keeping the heat on us for a day or so, he let it go.

We learned that we would be a part of the new XXIX Tactical Air Command being formed from personnel of the IXTAC, commanded by Major General Elwood "Pete" Quesada and from XIXTAC, our former unit, commanded by Major General Otto P. Weyland. Our new commander was Brigadier General Richard E. Nugent. The new command included about 200 officers, the majority of them having the rank of major, or higher. After two weeks in St.Quentin, we moved to Arlon, Belgium, and set up operations in a schoolroom in a monastery on a hill on the edge of town. Lieutenant Don Baldwin and I were given a room on the fourth floor to store our clothes and other gear, but we and other officers slept and had our meals in a downtown hotel about six blocks away. We resumed controller operations and were set up on regular shifts round the clock, as before.

In a letter to home in early October, I wrote that Arlon was

Operations Map Room Control Center-Lt. Col. Grossetta, Officer on Duty

a nice little town, situated on the southwest border of Luxembourg, that the townspeople spoke French, but the hotel manager and a few others spoke English. The hotel had a modern glass front, a nice cafe and steam heat. There was no heat in the school, but some stoves were being brought in. It was the first place where we were able to have our laundry done.

Allied commanders formulated a battle plan that would be followed until victory in May. It called for a battle line running north to south, with the British Second Army supported by the Royal Air Force at the north position. The Ninth Army would be on their right flank, supported by our XXIX TAC. On our right flank would be the First Army supported by XIX TAC, with the Third Army supported by IX TAC on the south.

One day while walking from the monastery to our hotel, I met a young girl and her housekeeper, who told me they were fasci-

"Rosellee"-XXIX TAC Controllers Operations Room-Maastricht, Holland

nated by their first sight of American troops. She gave me a small picture, and on the back she wrote, "Elaine Marie Le Pelletier De Glatigny, Chateau de Salvert A Venille (Maine et Louire)." We were in Arlon less than a month, and then moved to Maastricht, where we stayed until spring.

WITH THE NINTH AIR FORCE IN MAASTRICHT, HOLLAND

About the end of October, we moved again, this time to Maastricht, Holland. We set up fighter control operations in a school building in town and were quartered in another monastery across the river from downtown. We were soon back to three shifts a day - 7:30 to noon, noon to 5:30 and 5:30 to dark. Little did we know that we would be in this location for most of the winter. With a worsening of the weather, frequent heavy snows, and a slowdown of flight operations, the momentum for eastward movement was almost static. The busiest activity was with the weather and A-2 Intelligence sections, which had to give daily briefings. On November 6, several of us had an afternoon off and took a guided tour of the hundreds of tunnels in Fort St. Pieter on a hill overlooking Maastricht. The hill had been used as a limestone quarry by the Romans about 70 A.D. and was often called the eighth wonder of the world. We noticed that there were names and hometowns of many U.S. servicemen scratched on the wall, and the guides gave us permission to add ours.

In mid-November, Colonel Burton M. Hovey, who had been commander of the 303rd Fighter Squadron, was promoted to brigadier general, so we had two generals in the TAC. While there, I saw several boys from home. T/Sgt. Louis Fisher contacted me and we got together for a short visit. And one day I ran into W.A. "Dub" Nance, a first lieutenant chaplain of the Army. A star basketball player at Paducah Junior College, he had been an assistant pastor at a Mayfield, Kentucky, Methodist church.

As December rolled around, rumors began circulating that the war might be over in a month or so. On December 12th, orders came, transferring Second Lieutenant James Keane and me to the Eighth Air Force for temporary liaison duty. I was assigned a jeep from the motor pool. We drove to our new post near the front lines, just southwest of Aachen, Germany, to a microwave early warning station. We were assigned to an SCR-584 control unit, a truck-mounted station for close control work. We were quartered in two small frame hotels, side by side, with other Eighth Air Force officers. One hotel contained the officer's mess and the other was the officer's lounge.

The Eighth officers had hired a local man to be janitor. His pay was all the cigarette butts he could get out of the ashtrays at the bar and around the tables. Late each evening he would sit at a table and remove the papers from the tobacco and pour the collection into a coffee can. He could use the tobacco for himself or sell it on the black market. He said one night's collection would bring $20, which was twice as much as he could earn elsewhere, working all week. The

Inscriptions received March 2001 from Rik Willemse, cave guide at Mt. Saint Peter, Maastricht.

control unit was about two miles away, on a hill in the middle of a field surrounded by lots of mud. On the north and south sides of the hill, there were two U.S. Army anti-aircraft field artillery units. There was a trench on the low side of the hill behind the truck door, for use in case there was an enemy attack.

Sequel: In March of 2001, I received a letter from a guide in the caves of Mount St. Peter, Maastricht. He wrote, "These caves are literally filled with historical inscriptions, some dating back to the 16th century. I am conducting research focusing on the names written by American soldiers, who visited the caves right after the liberation of the town of Maastricht on Sept.14, 1944, to find out what happened to these people. For instance, whether they survived the war. This part of the investigation is conducted with the close cooperation of the American Military Cemetery in Maastricht. Your name, or maybe that of a relative, was written on the wall. I would like to know if you are the person in question. Attached is a digital picture I took. (Signed) Rik Willemse."

His email address was in his letter, so I sent him an answer, letting him know that I am that person and still alive and kicking. We have become regular correspondents and I have found him some of the information he is seeking. He has promised me a copy of his book, when completed. He 'phoned me March 24, 2002 to wish me a happy 88th birthday. (The Capt. C.M. McCauley, whose name is written above mine, was one of our controllers and took several of us to the cave that day.)

THE BATTLE OF THE BULGE

Jimmy Kean and I were still on temporary duty with the Eighth Air Force near Aachen when the Germans began their big east push, which became known as "The Battle of the Bulge." It happened early the morning of December 16,1944. Jimmy and I were on duty with two other Eighth men at the SDR-584, when we heard the roar of approaching aircraft east of us. Their blips appeared on our screen momentarily, as they made a strafing pass at our site. We made a scrambling dive out the door for the trench, which was too small for all four of us. I was blocked out by one of the others and went skittering down the slope in the snow. Fortunately, none of us was hit and damage to the site was minimal. Both anti-aircraft units opened up as the planes flew overhead. They were over and gone so quickly that we could not tell if they were ME-109s or FW-190s. We were too busy trying to get to the trench to be interested in identification. Most of the action all during the "Bulge" was a few miles north of our position. Later that morning another wave of enemy planes flew over, but they were so close to the ground there was no warning. They did not strafe us, but had a bigger target in mind. The batteries on each side of us were kept busy and continued to fire at every plane that flew near us, going or coming, both ours or theirs. An order about 11a.m. came through for all batteries to cease fire, but they were trigger-happy and let loose several times after the order came. We heard several of our pilots talking to other

Lt. Gen. William Simpson-Commander Ninth Army; Lt. Gen. Lewis Brereton-Commander Ninth Air Force; Brig. Gen. Richard Nugent-Commander XXIX TAC

pilots saying sarcastically, "Disregard that flak — it's friendly."

The 38 German divisions that struck along a fifty-mile front on December 16,1944 were halted by the Allies by December 27, despite heavy snowfall and dark overcast skies most of the time. This prevented our aircraft from providing air cover for our ground forces. Then on the first day of 1945, the Luftwaffe made large scale strafing raids against Allied airfields in Belgium and Holland, and destroyed a large number of British and American planes. But with the "Battle of the Bulge" over by the end of January, the Allies had won the battle of the skies. Our planes were able to concentrate on destroying the web of railroad track and marshalling yards that had kept the enemy supplied with vital needs. By the end of February, as the battle line moved over to the Roer River, our headquarters began a series of moves that would find us in Braunsweig when the Germans surrendered on May 9.

Our first move was to Munchen-Gladbach, about 100 kilometers north of Aachen. We set up operations in an existing Quonset hut and we officers moved our belongings into a row of small brick buildings that had been recently vacated by enemy troops. Most were damp and dirty, without heat or lights. Don Baldwin and I selected one of the cleaner ones, which still had straw on the floor, and had some windows missing. It looked like a stall for horses. But after hosing down and cleaning it, we made it livable. We were required to wear helmets and side arms. We hauled water and used our helmets for shaving and washing. It was quite a change from the quarters we had in Maastricht. With a week or so, we moved to Haltern, on the site of a former German boys camp, where our living conditions were much better.

There was a large lake near our operations that we would visit on our off hours. Across the lake was a black four-story frame warehouse, which we discovered was filled with kayaks. Most were not usable, as they were full of bullet holes. We did find a few that were and took them over on the bank near operations. We painted names on several and paddled around the lake a few times while we

Our Home-
Munchen-
Gladbach

were there. One evening while I was on duty, someone tapped me on the shoulder and asked if I was Lieutenant White from Paducah, Kentucky. Standing there was a sergeant with an Eighth Air Force patch on his flight jacket. He told me he was Marshall Nemer from Chicago and had married Marcia Finkel, a Paducah girl. His B-17 bomber had been shot up and he had bailed out and landed nearby, and had been brought to our headquarters. Earlier, on a stroll to the lake, he spotted a kayak marked "Barron White, Home Port, Paducah, Ky." I had a nice chat with him, but could not leave my post, so did not get a chance to visit longer with him. He was fed and given a place to sleep, and then the next day was sent back to his outfit in England. After the war we both came to Paducah, live in the same area, see each other at Rotary on Wednesdays, and remain good friends to this day. (note: Marshall died June 2002)

MUNSTER-GUTERSLOH

By April, the momentum of the push east increased rapidly and we were on the move about every week. We moved about 100 kilometers east to Munster, up to now the largest German city we had occupied. Munster, with a population over 200,000 people had been a target for the air forces for several months, and the rail lines, marshalling yards and enemy communication center had been destroyed. The Army selected a four-block area in the center of town, encircled it with barbed wire fencing and moved all inhabitants out and moved our troops into all the homes, with all furnishings kept intact. Every house was posted with a list of instructions to our men to neither remove nor destroy anything inside the home under a severe penalty for any violation. Everyone going out of the compound was checked before being permitted to pass. No citizens were permitted inside the fenced area during our stay.

This gave us our nicest quarters yet. Six of us had a nice suite of rooms with kitchen, laundry facilities, and indoor toilets. We enjoyed the hot water and took baths every night — a luxury we had not had for months. But we were soon on the move again with our next stop at Gutersloh, about 50 kilometers east of Munster. We were back to living in bombed-out buildings. Like most towns we saw as we drove from post to post, this city of 78,000 inhabitants was reduced to ruins, with the roads in and out cleared of debris, so vehicles could get through.

BRAUNSCHWEIG

On May 4,1944, I wrote home, "Guess you have been reading about German mass surrenders here and there. One day on the road to our next post, we passed hundreds of enemy troops of all ranks in their own uniforms and vehicles. They were driving to U.S. and British P.O.W. collection camps. It was an amazing sight to see - miles and miles of nothing but German troops and vehicles with only a few American guards miles apart. At one point, we came to an intersection where a German truck had broken down, blocking movement, with a German officer directing traffic. When he saw our jeep with two American officers, he cleared the way for us and gave us a snappy salute and waved us through. Some of the trucks were just limping along, in poor running condition. With their gasoline supply exhausted, many vehicles had wood-burning boilers mounted on the back, converted to furnish fuel. We arrived at our next location, Braunschweig, about 160 kilometers due west of Berlin, and set up operations in the airport buildings that were still standing. Officers were housed in three two-story buildings across the street from the airport entrance. The families who lived there were being evacuated, and were understandably upset, angry and tearful, afraid that they would not only lose their homes, but all their possessions. After we were settled in, several of the owners posted themselves in front of the buildings to protest, in case any of their goods were removed. To placate their fears, several of them were hired as housekeepers. From then until the end of hostilities, we were kept busy working shifts daily as our pilots performed surveillance and training missions."

TUESDAY, MAY 8, 1945-VE DAY

With the end of the war in Europe, I wrote "The wildest celebration that you can imagine happened. Radio programs broadcast speeches by Prime Minister Winston Churchill, George VI, the King of England, and U.S. President Harry S. Truman (whose birthday was May 8). Last night, when the official announcement was made, a noisy although brief celebration took place. Some old German fireworks were set off and for about an hour around midnight the sky was brilliantly lit. Our troops held an impromptu Fourth of July of our own. The sound of weapons being fired went on until most of the troops had fired off all of their ammunition. It was not safe to be out on the street with all the bullets whizzing around. Our team was on duty from midnight until dawn and claimed the distinction of pulling the last shift of the war. All day Tuesday, our five fighter groups put on an air show. Many were "hot-dogging" it and performing acrobatics never seen or permitted by Air Force pilots. Midday, a German FW-200 four-motored transport flew in from Norway with its crew of eight to surrender. Our control officer drove a jeep out to accept their surrender, but they refused to do so and asked that an officer of equal grade, major or higher, be sent out, which was done. Later that day several other aircraft flew in and surrendered. After things settled down, we began a training program, which kept us occupied. Everyone wondered when orders would come through to send us home. We submitted applications for leaves of absence, but with so many on file it was hard to know when it might come through. Things were relatively quiet for several weeks. Our leave applications came through and we flew to England for a nice week visiting friends. I was given a temporary duty assignment to go to Brussels and pick up the TAC's monthly supply of beverages, supplied under reverse lend-lease arrangements. I flew over and rode back in the truck. While there I ran into an old friend from home, Harold "Hoppy" Futrell, there on R&R. We had dinner at a nearby nightclub and ran into another Paducah friend, John McNutt, also on R&R. We had a few enjoyable hours together, comparing our service experiences. The next day the company supplies sergeant and I started the drive back with the goods. We stopped at Maastricht, spent the night at the monastery, and drove through Aachen, crossed the Rhein at Cologne and on the autobahn to Braunschweig."

FURSTENFELDBRUCH

On July 12, the entire XXIX TAC flew to Furstenfeldbruch, in the Bavarian Alps near Munich. I was fortunate to get to fly down in General Nugent's C-47 and sat in a nice, soft, comfortable armchair. We took over the abandoned airfield and we controllers were immediately assigned shifts to handle the traffic at the field. We were given a "Biscuit" gun, with a red and green control light, a portable radio and a small vehicle with a glass dome. We were told to park the vehicle in the middle of the field and talk to all aircraft flying to the field and supply them with any necessary information. This was awkward at first, for we were given no information or other instructions. Four of us were given a nice room in the officer's building. We also had a nice balcony overlooking the club veranda. The officer's mess and clubrooms were downstairs. We had German waitresses and music by a German string ensemble during noon and evening meals.

This airbase covered a large area. Some of the buildings had hallways that looked as though they were a mile long. There was an adjacent swimming pool, several tennis courts, and a nice gym. A number of Bavarian men wearing lederhosen tended the flower garden and the shrubbery. We were hoping to get a chance to fly to Italy and Switzerland, but this never happened. While we were there, I received a nice card from Sam Sloan, my Paducah insurance friend, who offered congratulations for my being promoted to captain.

A week later, we moved our equipment off the runway into the tower, which was atop the four-story building on the edge of the

158

This was traffic control at Firstenfeldbruch. Germany at XXIX TAC Airstrip-Ninth Air Force Controller Captain Walt Anderson on 8-hour shift armed with radio-biscuit gun-45 revolver.

field. We had a glass enclosed eight-foot square room with windows floor to ceiling with an all-around view for miles. There was a porch all around the tower and arranged so we could climb on top of the tower and sit in a chair and control from there. We still used our portable radio and biscuit gun. We knew our stay there would not be of long duration. We started mailing boxes with extra clothes and souvenirs home. We had accumulated a lot of extra "stuff" along the way and needed to cut down what we would take home. On off hours we scouted around the countryside.

We discovered a beautiful golf course at nearby Feldafing and managed a few rounds with Colonel McGehee, Colonel McGlinn and Captain Perpich. We got clubs and balls from Special Services. Balls were scarce and the ones we got were used and scruffy. The Germans didn't play much golf. We were told there were only 26 courses in Germany. We were told that the course had been taken over by the Third Cavalry and was for use by Army personnel only. While there, Glen Miller's AEF band flew over and gave us a good one-hour show outdoors. We enjoyed the good old American music. The band featured their great pianist, Mel Powell, singer Johnny Desmond, and Ray McKinley who directed. We began to have more USO shows, probably because Munich was right in the center of their circuit. Bob Hope and his group came and put on a good show.

THE LAST ASSIGNMENT
THEN HOME

FURSTENFELDBRUCH TO
CORONADO, CALIFORNIA

On August 11, we were excited to find the following Special Orders posted on the bulletin board near the mess hall. "The following named officers and enlisted men, XXIX Tactical Air Command, are placed on detached service, Amphibious Training Command, Coronado, CA, under Project...for the purpose of receiving indoctrination on Navy methods of aircraft control.

Personnel will proceed to Orley Air Field, (Paris) reporting to Captain Fields, not later than 1200 hours, 12 August 45, for the purpose of returning to the ZI (zone of the interior) by air under "Green" Project. At Orley Field, further instructions will be issued by Captain Fields. Major Clyde McCauley is appointed senior officer in charge. Baggage limitation sixty-five pounds." This included eight officers from headquarters squadron, sixteen officers from the

XXIX control group and four officers and eleven enlisted men from the 433 Fighter Control Squadron. The order was by command of Brigadier General Nugent, and signed by Colonel Dyke F. Meyer, Chief of Staff.

We packed up our gear and took off early the next morning aboard a Military Air Transport Service plane for USAFE St. Germaine, (Paris) after an emotional session of goodbyes. It would be the last time we saw many people who had become close friends after serving together for over a year. On August 16, we were put under new orders to fly to the United States. We took off from Orley Field in a four-engine propeller-driven plane with our baggage piled between the pilots and us. We sat along the sides in bucket seats with canvas bottoms. Another plane like ours accompanied us for the whole trip. We made a brief stop in Lisbon, Portugal, took off for the 800-mile trip to Santa Maria Island in the Azores for refueling and then on to Newfoundland, 1,000 miles northwest.

About halfway there, we heard a special news report announcing the surrender of the Japanese and end of the war in the Pacific. When we landed around midnight at Gander Field, a wild celebration was in progress. Normal processing was impossible, with everyone dancing, shouting, drinking, and not caring about working. We finally were able to get fed and off to bed. It was not until we landed at Newfoundland that I discovered that one of the pilots on the other plane was "Bub" Purky, a Paducah boy, and longtime friend. The next morning at breakfast, we gorged ourselves on fresh eggs and real milk, something we had missed during our years overseas. We re-boarded our plane and flew to New Castle Air Base, Wilmington, Delaware, where new orders were cut to have us proceed to Coronado, California, and report upon arrival to P.O. Williams, commander of air support amphibious training. After lunch, we caught a bus to LaGuardia Field, and boarded an American Airlines commercial flight and made stops at Washington, D.C., Knoxville, Nashville, Memphis, Dallas, Ft. Worth, Tucson, Phoenix and Long Beach before landing at San Diego. We rode a shuttle to the U.S. Naval Amphibious Training Base. We were checked in and given lodging in the officer's barracks.

We soon began a series of programs to prepare us for being sent to a station somewhere in the Pacific. We liked our stay at the Naval base. The grounds and flowers were immaculate, kept that way by several dozen German prisoners of war, who had been there for months. We enjoyed the good food, leisurely days, with warm sunshine and excellent recreational facilities. Although we were in school for over a month, we had a good feeling that we would not be sent to the Pacific. It was like being in college. Major McCauley, our senior officer, aware of our desire to get a leave before any further moves, kept in frequent touch with his superior, Colonel Anthony V. Grossetta in Washington. I had requested that I be sent to Chicago to start my leave, as my mother was visiting my sister there that summer. It was not until late September that we received leave orders, signed by a Lieutenant Sanders, assistant air adjutant general under General "Hap" Arnold. My orders indicated that I would travel to Fort Dix, New Jersey, for my flight to Paducah. Apparently the separation center decided that would be the nearest point to Kentucky. But it didn't take long to get that corrected and I finally received orders to report to the Separation Center, Sixth Service Command, Fort Sheridan, Illinois. I flew by commercial airline to Chicago, spent the night with family and then reported to Fort Sheridan to get my 30-day leave papers. As I filled out the forms the duty officer said, "Hey! You have accumulated enough points to be discharged." I could not believe it, but quickly decided to get out. I was given a choice of staying in the reserves or getting out completely. I asked which door was out? I returned to my family in Chicago and told them the good news. My brother Harry had been able to get a three-day pass from the Army base in Great Falls, Montana, and we had a delightful family reunion. Then a ride on the Illinois Central train to Kentucky and back home, a civilian again. Three days later, back to work at Petter Supply Company, where I would stay until retirement in 1989.

WARTIME ENCOUNTERS

In letters home during my time in the service, I wrote that I saw a number of Paducahans at various places. I mentioned most in passing and didn't give much detail. At the risk if being redundant, I will recount my remembrances of those I happened to meet.

The two local boys who were inducted with me were George "Brownie" Wedel and "Buck" Willingham. I don't think I ever knew Buck's real name. We were together at the Evansville examination center, the Ft. Benjamin Harrison reception center, and at Jefferson Barracks in St. Louis. We parted from there. While at "Ft. Ben," one of the permanent party personnel was Arvin Bunger, who later married Manie Young and was in our "Barbershoppers" chorus in later years.

While in officer candidate school in 1943 at Miami Beach, and billeted at the Peter Miller Hotel, I discovered that my squadron officer was 2nd. Lt. Ralph M. Aland, who had married Jeanette Wolfson, a Paducah girl, whose mother owned and operated Wolfson's Dress Shop, where Aunt Lottie White worked for many years. I kept seeing a blue convertible with McCracken County, Kentucky, license plates parked in front of the hotel and when I asked our sergeant, he told me it belonged to Lt. Aland. When I got permission to speak to him, I told him that I knew Jeanette. He displayed little or no interest in furthering the relationship, which was disappointing, for I wanted to see her if only for a moment or two. By that time, I had been in the Army for ten months and would have liked to see anyone from home, especially a pretty girl like Jeanette. Aland was an Alabama boy, Jewish as was Jeanette, and returned to his home after the war. I never saw either of them again.

While stationed at the Orlando School of Applied Tactics, right after I was graduated from officer's school as a second lieutenant, I encountered Paducahan "Soapie" Harris, who was an armament officer over at the main base. I knew who he was, but that was all. We got together for a golf game, and that was the last time I saw him and don't know what ever happened to him. A few weeks before

I left Orlando for New York, I learned that Pete Langstaff was stationed nearby, so I phoned him and we met at the officer's club for a nice visit and later both went to the post library to write a few letters. Pete was regular Army, a graduate of the military academy at West Point. In 1925, when our family moved into the upstairs apartment at the Langstaff home at 731 Kentucky Avenue, all of us were quite young. I was eleven, and Pete was seven or eight. Although he was younger, we played together on a number of occasions. After Pete left the service, he settled down in Florida out in the "boondocks," liked being outdoors and to experience rugged activities.

One summer Pete hiked the entire length of the Appalachian Trail, a 1,995-mile footpath that stretches from Maine to Springer Mountain in Georgia. He walked it alone, sometimes stopping on weekends to get mail and supplies and occasionally driving home and returning to where he left off. Some years later he showed us slides of his walk. He also led a team on a horse and wagon trip from east to west across the northwest part of the United States. There were about eight people, most of whom were women. Pete made infrequent trips home to visit his mother until her death. On one such trip, he started out to walk the Natchez Trace, which begins at Grand Rivers, Kentucky, and goes through the Land Between The Lakes and continues to Natchez, Mississippi. After a few days, however, he got so covered with deer ticks that he became quite ill and had to stop. He was sick for more than a week, and then decided to return home and abandon his plan to walk the Trace. A year or so later, he died quite suddenly, and many of us suspect it had something to do with all those deer tick bites.

Also while at the Orlando officer's club, I ran into George Brievogel, who was a second lieutenant, flying B-25 twin-engine bombers at a nearby air base. He was some younger than I. He and his family lived between 16th and 17th streets on Harrison. He or his parents would come to Dad's grocery at the corner of 16th and Madison almost every day. George was a typical "hot shot" pilot, with the crushed cap, the silk scarf and the swagger. I don't know what ever happened to him or whether he survived.

While stationed in Norfolk with the First Air Defense Wing,

I knew that several Paducahans in the Navy were stationed there. I phoned Forrest Ladd, who had lived near us on North 23rd Street and ran around with Harry and our crowd. I was with him one time when a few Paducah boys got together. I recall Oscar Hank being there. Seems there were two others, but I can't recall who they were. I know they weren't close friends. All those I saw were Naval ensigns. I did run across L.V. Bean, who was a lieutenant colonel and was post engineer at Camp Lee, Virginia. L.V. had been the Paducah city manager a few years back and his son Vimont went to Tilghman and ran with some of our group.

While crossing the Atlantic on the *Queen Mary*, ten of our squadron, all second lieutenants, were assigned to be traffic officers for all decks. I was instructed to select six staff sergeants from the roster to assist me. My area was the third deck and I was charged with the responsibility of seeing that all men on my deck got down the stairs to meals quickly and on time. The meal schedules for each deck were different and staggered, as the dining area could accommodate only a few hundred at a time. There were about 15,000 men on board. When the six sergeants reported to me for instructions, I noticed that one of them looked familiar. When I rechecked my roster I discovered that he was my first sergeant at Parks Air College while I was there. I was student acting first sergeant and had to report to him every day. He was a former baseball umpire and was tough on us. Most all sergeants had to be tough and lots of them were mean and took advantage of their authority, which could not be questioned. I remember many soldiers saying that if they ever had an opportunity to get back at their sergeants, that they would give them a double dose of what they had to take from them. That was my normal reaction, too, but when I saw my sergeant, I was genuinely glad to see him and treated him with the utmost kindness and courtesy. And he appreciated it, too, and was most helpful to me all the way across.

Before I left the States, I met Dorothy Willis, a Navy nurse, who told me that she had lived on Fountain Avenue. I had seen her in Paducah, but didn't know who she was.

Once while in the Willard Hotel in Washington, D.C., I saw

General George C. Marshall come in the door and walk down the hall past me. I was in uniform, sitting in a chair in the corridor and for a moment I froze, not remembering if I was supposed to snap to attention, jump to "parade rest," or rise and salute. I just sat there as he strode by, eyes straight ahead. To him, I was just part of the furniture. I also ran into Nolan Fisher and Bill Ryan, Army officers stationed in the Washington, D.C., area. Nolan and his brother Gene, had operated a filling station at the corner of 7th and Broadway, and later became successful homebuilders. Bill stayed in the Army until he retired, still lives in the Washington, D.C., area and occasionally visits in Paducah. I recall that when I was on the Jaycees committee to recruit candidates for the Army Air Force, Bill submitted an application for the flying cadet program. He was accepted and went through pilot training and flew missions during WWII.

The first Paducahan I encountered after landing in England was Joe Whedon, who graduated a year ahead of me at Tilghman. Joe had gone to St. Mary's until he got to high school, but as St. Mary's didn't have a football team, Joe transferred to ATHS. He became a regular end on the varsity squad and lettered every year. Later he married Mary Elisabeth "Bill" Dunbar, and owned and operated a TV and appliance business under the name of Major Distributors. When I saw him in England, I had been overseas about six months and he had just come over within the prior two weeks. His mail hadn't caught up with him and when I told him that he had a new baby girl, it was the first he had heard about it. I had received a news clipping from home a few days earlier. As I remember, I was stationed with the British at Stanmore, Sussex, a few miles north of London when I ran into him on a quiet street. However, years later when we met at a restaurant in Paducah, Joe said he remembered us meeting at Piccadilly Circus, which I think is not right. I didn't question his memory and now wonder about mine. When I referred to my WWII letter written to mother June 14,1944, my letter read, "Yesterday while visiting in XXXXXXXXXX (X'd out by censor). When I researched my orders, the town was Stanmore. When I heard that Louis Fisher and Bob Hassman were in England, I found where they were stationed and phoned them and tried to arrange a meeting place. I never did meet Bob, but did see Louis after we got on the continent.

In July 1944, Mr. Petter wrote and asked me to look up his brother-in-law, Joe Phillips, who had been a news correspondent in Italy and who was then a liaison officer with the British Air Ministry. I went to his London office and had nice chat with him. He took my phone number and indicated he and Mrs. Phillips would phone me and have me out to dinner, but I never heard from them. The first homeboy I encountered after I got to France was Harry (H.J.) Livingston. He had learned where I was, around St. Mere Eglise, which was around 85 kilometers from his station, so he borrowed a jeep, drove up to our place and we spent the better part of the day together. This was in August 1944.

In November while in Holland, I found where Louis Fisher was stationed, so drove over and spent the evening and night and drove back the next day. Then I ran into W.A. "Dub" Nance, who was a first lieutenant chaplain in the Army. Dub had been a basketball star at PCC and an assistant pastor at Vivian Waldrop's Mayfield Methodist Church. In one letter home, I'd mentioned seeing him at the Union Station in Washington, D.C., while there visiting Mary Bayne Lackey. One day while quartered in Braunsweig, Germany, I was walking down a street in the town square and saw Barbara Rutter 's husband, Bill Acker, who had been a teller at Citizens Bank for years. I crossed over, greeted him warmly and proceeded to tell him how glad I was to see him. His only response was, "Yeah." He acted as if I had just seen him at 4th and Broadway, in front of the bank, and showed no warmth or interest at all. That was his nature, though, as he was always quiet, non-committal, and reserved even while working.

While on leave in Brussels, Belgium, I saw Hoppy Futrell coming out the door of the hotel as I was going in. Hoppy, a first lieutenant was there on R&R, just like I was. We had a pleasant afternoon together, talking about old times at home when we were both members of the "Harahan Hoboes," as we boys who lived on Harahan Boulevard called ourselves. We decided to have dinner together at the Carso Club, a favorite and popular nightclub there in

Brussels. We had just finished our meal and were sitting back enjoying a drink and watching the couples on the dance floor. Hoppy suddenly said, "Look at that bald-headed man out there on the floor, dancing with that girl in the blue skirt. From the back, it looks just like John McNutt." And, sure enough, it was. When he turned around and saw us he came over and sat with us and we spent the evening together. John was another "Harahan Hobo," although he lived on Park Avenue near 18th Street. He was in Harry's school class and had been a reporter at the *Paducah Sun-Democrat* before he went into the service. The next day, John had to leave and rejoin his outfit in France. John was a first lieutenant and later worked for the New York Times. After John left Brussels, Hoppy and I stayed over another day together.

There were a number of people I met while in the service who were from towns around Paducah. They always knew someone I knew, so we usually had a lot to talk about. I didn't record their names so couldn't look up any of them when I returned home. Being in the service gave me an opportunity to see, be with or meet personally a lot of movie stars and other famous people. We saw Bob Hope's show at Brookley Field in Mobile, Alabama, at OCS in Miami, and in Germany. At the USO show in Germany, I was asked

Barron and Hoppy Futrell-Brussels, Belgium-1945

to drive some of his party around. The only well-known name in my vehicle was Jerry Colonna, who rode up front with me. Hope was in our caravan, several cars behind us. Other USO performers who were billeted with us while putting on their show were Marlene Dietrich, Brian Ahern, Lunt & Fontanne and Jascha Heifetz. None were there at the same time, all being on separate tours. Once at a movie in London, the theater had just darkened as the show started. At that moment, two big bulky soldiers came to my aisle and took seats just to my left. I couldn't tell much about them, but when the lights were turned back on, I recognized that one was Joe Louis, heavyweight champion boxer. Our 29th TAC had just moved from Munchen-Gladbach, across the Rhein River to Haltern, a small village near Dusseldorf, which had been practically obliterated by the Eighth Air Force's B-17 and B-24 bombers. That is where I met Marshall Nemer.

TALK GIVEN THE PADUCAH ROTARY CLUB
JUNE 15,1994
AFTER OUR RETURN FROM THE
50TH ANNIVERSARY OF D-DAY
AT NORMANDY, FRANCE

Zelma and I returned last Thursday night from a 10-day tour of England and France. We spent a hectic four days touring the Normandy coast and visiting the five invasion beaches from Sword to Utah. Our hotel was at Harfluor, a small village near La Havre, on the east side of all the beaches, so we spent a lot of time on the bus getting to and from the sites each day. With the 50,000-plus veterans there, (our group consisted of 40 busloads) for the first three days, traffic was bumper to bumper, and when we got off the main roads and drove through the small villages to get to the beaches, it was pure gridlock. At every village we visited; Caen, Bayeaux, St. Lo, Carentan, and St. Mere-Eglise, we were joyously welcomed by crowds of local citizens, waving American and French flags. Every village and house along the way was covered with banners and flags of all the Allied nations. On Sunday we witnessed the parachute drop at St. Lo by 50 WWII veterans and by 700 of the 82nd and the 102nd Airborne.

On D-Day, we started out at 5:30 a.m. joined our assigned caravan of about 20 busses at Caen, and were given a police escort all the way to Utah Beach, where we were scheduled to take part in the day's services. At every road intersection along the way gendarmes stood guard from dawn to dusk. We had to walk about a half mile from the field where the 500-plus buses had to park. We joined a long line of people walking toward the beach and had to go through a security check about halfway there, to make sure we were not carrying grenades or other weapons. Three tiers of stadium seats had been set up in front of the podium, with a plastic canopy to protect us in case of rain. We were able to get good seats (about an 8-iron away) from the center of the activities. We sat just behind the roped-off section of seats reserved for members of Congress and their wives (paid for by U.S. taxpayers).

The D-Day ceremony was very impressive and very moving. When it was announced that President Clinton would be about ten minutes late, there were some light scattered boos, but he was given a very rousing ovation when he and French President Francois Mitterand arrived. A 21-gun salute started the proceedings, followed by the national anthems of the United States and France. President Mitterand made the official welcoming address and Secretary Perry introduced the President, who made a very eloquent speech. He asked all veterans who had served in the invasion to stand up and be recognized. He said, "You men preserved our liberty and the freedoms we have enjoyed for the past 50 years. You went willingly and without question in answer to your country's need. You saved the world from tyranny, hypocrisy and fear. We are the children of your sacrifice." He then asked for a few moments of silence for those who had made the supreme sacrifice, the 9,300 buried nearby in the American Military Cemetery at Colleville. In the afternoon, we attended the ceremonies at the American Military Cemetery at

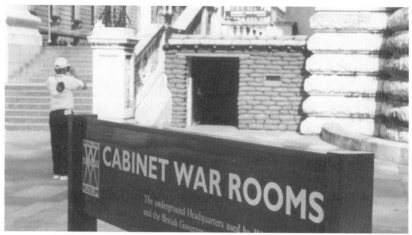

Churchill Underground Headquarters during World War II-London

Omaha Beach, where heads of state and other dignitaries from twelve of the Allies attended.

All in all, there was so much to see, and due to the tremendous crowds and a lack of time, we missed a lot of the activities. We wanted to spend more time at each location we visited - time to read the inscriptions on the many monuments, to walk the beaches, and to have time to drink in the atmosphere. It was an historic moment, a commemoration of the mightiest amphibious assault in the history of man and one we will never forget. Never again, will so many veterans of a war get together at one time at one place. I felt proud and humble to have been a part of it.

THOMAS C. TERRELL
Lieutenant Colonel USAF (Retired)

I became aware of Tom Terrell when he starred on the Tilghman High School and Paducah Junior College basketball teams in the late 1930s and early 1940s. When it became evident that the United States was going to enter the war, Tom was among the first to apply for flight training. When the U.S. declared war after the attack on Pearl Harbor, 5,000 men and women from McCracken

Ed Hank and Barron White-American Military Cemetery-Omaha Beach, France

County entered military service in this country and overseas, found their lives disrupted and were separated from their homes and families for the duration of the war, some never to return. When it was over, a large number of those who returned to civilian status had married and never came back to Paducah to live. Tom was among those who did just that and I lost track of him for a few years.

Tom never lost his interest and affection for his hometown. His sister, "Trace" Wells, still lived in the old homeplace on North 36th Street and Tom visited her several times a year. And although Trace died two years ago, he still comes. Her granddaughter maintains the family home and Tom still has his old room there when he visits. He enjoys going with me to our Wednesday Rotary meetings, getting up a golf game, going to Grace Episcopal on Sundays and visiting a number of long-time friends including, John Bryan, Emmett Holt, and Bill Black. Since he retired, golf has been high on his priority list and he plays courses wherever he goes. His son, Tom Terrell III, who earlier was an aircraft pilot for Crounse Corporation here, lives in Baton Rouge, Louisiana, and is a scratch golfer and they get together frequently.

Tom's military service record is most impressive. After completing 36 weeks of primary, basic and advanced flying courses, he earned his wings and was commissioned a second lieutenant on

Thomas C. Terrell-Lt. Col., USAF

November 3, 1943. Tom had 40 combat missions against the Japanese in the Philippines, flying B-24 bombers from Anguan, Palau Island, as a part of the 494th Group, 7th Air Force. After World War II ended, he took additional training, which included four weeks of IBM machines, 11 weeks of nuclear weapons instructor courses and related weapons schooling, and twenty-two weeks of aircraft transition training in B-24, B-50, and B-47 bombers. He said, "The B-50 was an improved version of the B-29. It had more reliable power, a higher vertical stabilizer (better stability) and nose wheel steering (a pilot's dream), also better radar."

He was assigned to SAC (Strategic Air Command) and sent to Roswell, New Mexico, and served with the 509th Bomb Wing, 15th Air Force. After 7 years he went with the 509th to Pease AFB, New Hampshire, 8th Air Force. At these two bases most of the flights were training missions. There were no armed bombs involved, although they did drop heavy training bombs to check accuracy and simulate combat conditions. During the Lebanon and Cuban crises, all SAC planes were fully armed, ready to go. There were about twenty other SAC wings. They could fly anywhere in the "lower 48," but usually stayed within 600 miles of their base. When he was offered a staff position in 1956, he accepted it. It required him to maintain flying status and stay current in the aircraft that the wing flew. His military duties included being responsible to the deputy commander for operations on all matters pertaining to the wing's emergency war orders and alert force; development of a smooth functioning operational organization, and he was responsible for the preparation and quality of the wing's war plan and the air crew knowledge thereof. He was in a position of great trust - a primary custodian of sensitive documents affecting national security. Also he was responsible for quality, content and presentation of material used to brief visiting officers on the wing's war plan. He held top security clearance. Rated as a command pilot with a total flying time of 5,300 hours, of which 1,365 hours was six-engine jet time, he served throughout World War II and later for 22 years and ten months, retiring in March 1965.

In April 1966, he started a new career with Eastern Airlines, Flight Operations Division, as manager of administration for flights standards, a position he held until he retired again in September 1987. I always look forward to his visits, for we have a good time together. He is always upbeat and eager to see and do all he can while here. His enthusiasm and exuberance are contagious and he makes friends wherever he goes. I consider Tom a dear close friend.

EMMETT L.HOLT
Colonel USAF (retired)

Emmett Holt was born in Paducah, November 1920 to Emmett and Hettie Holt. His father was a former McCracken County sheriff and city commissioner of safety. Emmett graduated from Tilghman High School and Paducah Junior College and was a student at UK one year before volunteering for the Air Corps. Emmett recalls, "I received my pilot's license in 1940, before I went into the service. Shortly after that three of us, Don Williams, Ralph Pryor and I, rented a three-place aircraft to go to a UK football game at Lexington, Kentucky. About 30 minutes out the engine quit and I had to make a forced landing in a cornfield. We never would have made it to the game, as I was already lost."

(Author's note-My brother Harry and I were in the same 1940 CAA class with Emmett. Others in the class were: Carmen Maxie, Frank Young, Allard Hardy, Carl Sears, Gene Morgan, O.E Garrett and Clifton Miller. The ground instructor was Lieutenant Dick DeVania. L.E. "Toogie" Galbraith was flight instructor. All flight training was at Howell Field on the Coleman Road.)

Emmett took pre-flight training at Maxwell Field, Alabama; primary training at Ocala, Florida; and basic training at Gunter Field, Alabama. Then he was sent to Lawrenceville, Illinois, for advanced training, where he received his wings and was commissioned a second lieutenant in class 43C. He was held in reserve until October 1942 when he was called to active service. He attended pursuit training at Brownsville, Texas; B-24 training at Smyrna, Tennessee; and C-46 training at Reno, Nevada. Emmett says, "I was qualified in every aircraft in the Air Force, except the B-17 and B-26."

He was assigned to the air transport command, ferry division and after months of delivering aircraft to various theaters, was assigned to the China-Burma-India theater, flying C-46s over the "Hump," the 500-mile run over the Himalayas, between India and China. He said while he was at Reno, he flew quite a bit as co-pilot with former Paducahan J.D. Payne, who was recalled to active duty from Eastern Airlines and became one of the first pilots to fly the hump as a member of the Flying Tigers.

Emmett was discharged after the war and accepted a position with the Civil Aeronautics Administration in New York. He was recalled to active duty for 90 days in September 1948 as an air traffic controller for the New York Air Traffic Center, to assist in the establishment of procedures and control of traffic for the Berlin Airlift. He reminisced about going over, "All the wheels from the regional office were around and I wondered what was up. It wasn't long until I found out. They were there to select men to go to Germany and control air traffic. We left Wednesday for Westover Field and landed in Germany Friday and five of us left immediately for Tempelhof Air Base, Berlin. We received a good briefing and the next afternoon were put on schedule, operating in the new control

Emmett Holt

position under the tower. I didn't believe that I would be controlling traffic in Berlin in less than a week."

During the Airlift, they had a lot of visitors at the ATC Center, including Prime Minister Clement Attlee and Bob Hope. Emmett said, "I was on duty the day that Charles Lindbergh paid us a visit. Any dignitary usually had escorts such as the base commander. I saw a lone man walking on the ramp. When he came in he said, 'Captain, I'm Charles Lindbergh. I understand that you are bringing in these aircraft once every three minutes. If you have time could you show me how you are doing it?' He talked to me quite a bit and asked the most penetrating questions of any individual that I had briefed."

Emmett remained there on active duty after the initial 90 days and was assigned to the AFCS group as group air traffic control officer, to establish and instruct a school for ASAFE controllers in Europe. He served a tour as an air traffic control specialist at Andrews Air Force Base, the USAF Systems Command Headquarters, Washington, D.C. Then he was assigned to the AFCS wing in Elmensdorf, Alaska, as an air control officer. At the conclusion of this tour, he was assigned to SAC as a pilot on a four-engine KC-97 Stratofreighter, delivering military troops and cargo here and abroad. When the Airway Modernization Board was established, he became one of the original members. He served a tour with the Bureau of Research and Development as an FAA systems research analyst. Then was reassigned to Air Force Headquarters as an air traffic control officer. He was selected as an alternate military member to the Community for European Airspace Coordination, headquartered at Weisbaden, Germany. He later also assumed the duties of the chief of air traffic control division of headquarters. His tour in Europe was curtailed and he was reassigned as the Department of Defense representative on the Advisory Committee on Air Traffic Control. Emmett retired with the rank of colonel in 1974, after serving 30 years in the military. He accumulated over 1,000 hours of flying time. His decorations include the Legion of Merit, Joint Services Commendation Medal, Air Force Commendation Medal, and the Army Commendation Medal.

He married Barbara Bockman, his childhood sweetheart, in 1951 and they have two sons, Jack and Bob. Barbara was able to be with him a part of the time when he was in Europe. She accompanied him one year while he served in Saudi Arabia, helping set up their communication and air control system. They moved back to Paducah and are spending their retirement years back home.

JOHN R. ILER
Captain U.S. Navy (Retired)

John Iler was born in Paducah on February 6, 1922. His parents were Virgil Brandon and Hettye Hayes Iler. He moved to Melber, Kentucky, with his mother due to his parents' separation, then returned to Paducah in 1937 and completed the last two years at Tilghman High School. He lived at 400 North 16th Street and worked during vacations and spare time for VanAart Florist. He attended Murray College from 1937 to 1942, majoring in physics. He worked as college photographer at Murray and at Paducah Boy Scout Camp during the summer months. He completed civil pilot's training in February 1942.

It was during the period of the late 30s and early 40s that I first met John. He and I shared the same hobbies - swimming, tennis and photography. We frequented the tennis courts at Barkley

Park regularly with Pershing Rogers, W.L Beasley, my brother Harry and others. John remembers the time we swept the snow off the courts to play one winter.

John entered the United States Navy as a flying cadet in May 1942. He took pre-flight training at the University of Iowa. After receiving his wings and commission in June 1932, he joined Patrol Squadron VP-72 at Kaneohe Bay, Oahu, and flew missions in PBY Catalinas. He participated in the Central Pacific campaigns from the Baker, Gilbert and Marshall islands. During this (June 1944) tour, he qualified as patrol plane commander in Catalina Flying Boats. He flew more than seventy missions and received a Letter of Commendation for open sea landing rescue of downed pilots in the Marshalls campaign. He received the Air Medal for the Gilberts campaign.

John returned to the U.S. in August 1944 and was promoted to lieutenant junior grade. He went through operational training in PB4Y Liberators as plane commander at Hutcheson, Kansas; Jacksonville, Florida; San Diego, California; and Kaneohe, Oahu.

In April 1945 he returned to the Pacific to join Patrol Bombing Squadron 117 in the Philippines, from where he flew patrols covering the South China Sea and Indo-China. The high point of this tour was a fifty-odd minute air battle, as nine assorted Japanese fighters kept him under constant attack while he made his attacks on shipping and dock installations, then withdrew to fly the 1,100 miles back to his base in the Philippines. He flew more than 35 patrols, received the Distinguished Flying Cross and five more Air

John Iler

Medals. The squadron was awarded the Presidential Unit Citation for operations in which sixty-three enemy aircraft were destroyed in the air and thousands of tons of enemy shipping were sunk. At the end of the war PVB-117 moved its base to the Marianas and flew weather reconnaissance missions before returning to the United States in November 1945. John was promoted to lieutenant in 1946. Ordered to the Training Command at Pensacola, he instructed in Flying Boats for a few months, then was assigned to the staff of the commander of naval air training bases, where he served as plane officer and aide to the commander. Departing Pensacola in December 1947, he completed fighter refresher training in Corsairs, and was assigned to the staff of the commander, Carrier Division SIX aboard the *USS Kearsage*, and served as assistant operations, navigator, and intelligence officer.

In February 1949, he joined the Navy's first jet squadron, Fighter Squadron 171, then flying F4-1 Phantoms and later received the first production P2H-1 Banshees. He served as supply, training and operations officer. In August 1949, John was one of two test pilots who flew F2H Banshees to an altitude of 51,000 to demonstrate intercept capability above the then accepted ceiling of 45,000 altitude. Despite flameouts on both planes, both were able to complete the mission and make the test a success. Reporting to the Naval Air Station Sanford, Florida, May 1951, he served as communications, assistant operations and operations officer. He was promoted to lieutenant commander June 1, 1953. From August 1953 to February 1954, he attended the U.S. Naval Post Graduate School at Monterey, California. Ordered to Anti-Submarine Development Squadron ONE March 1954, he served until March 1956 as plans and liaison officer while flying as plane commander in Marlin Flying Boats and jet-assisted Neptune Patrol Boats. He flew the operational test on the nuclear depth charge Betty. After completing all-weather intercept training, he joined Fighter Squadron 31 as acting commanding officer. Later, he served as executive officer until January 1957, when he was ordered to Fighter Squadron 43 as commanding officer. Operating swept-wing F9F Cougars throughout 1957, VF-43 was assigned F8U Crusaders.

1,000 Miles an Hour-Commander John R. Iler of Paducah recently flew his F8U crusader more than 1,000 miles an hour. Commander Iler is commanding officer of Navy Fighter Squadron 43, known as the Fighting Falcons. His squadron is operating the F8U, which not only is the fastest carrier-based fighter, but is one of the fastest operational aircraft in the world.

Following his detachment from VF-43, Commander Iler reported to the Air War College. He was promoted to commander August 1957. He had flown over 5,000 hours, and spent nearly seven months of his life in the air. He attended War College in 1958-59, then spent two years in the Navy Research and Development Test and Evaluation "Budget Business" at the Pentagon, 1959-61 of which he said, "It was one hell of a grind."

In late 1961, he was ordered to the *USS Forrestal* as navigator for about eight months, and then became operations officer until 1962. He returned from the Mediterranean, where the Forrestal was deployed, and in 1963 became aide to Four-Star Vice Chief of Naval Operations Ricketts. John said news of the death of Admiral Ricketts in 1964 was a great loss to him, both as a friend and future booster. He attended the Industrial College 1964-65 and took the George Washington University MBA on the side. Following this school, he was ordered to Strategic Plans Division in the Pentagon, where, he said, "I pushed JCS papers in nuclear warfare planning for 2 years. I had one of the most interesting aviation careers of anyone I know. I made both the deep draft list and the major command list, but I think I missed an attack carrier command due to my squadron tours in big planes. At the time, the deep draft ship command was not making many admirals. The multi-engine squadrons hurt me for command of an attack carrier and for possible flag rank. So I turned down my deep draft command and retired at age 46."

John married Deane Morgan of Paducah on March 18,1951. They have three children, John Robert Iler Jr., David Lorin Iler and Patricia Kelly Iler. John and Deane live in Arlington, Virginia, where John remains an avid and active tennis player. During his years of active duty when on leave, and after retirement, he would usually come every year to visit his old hometown. He had "PADUCAH" proudly displayed beneath his name on the plane.

BACK TO AN ACTIVE CIVILIAN LIFE

CHARITY LEAGUE FOLLIES

The Charity League was organized in 1932 by a group of sixteen young society women. In 1929 and 1930 they sponsored a dance called the Snowball, to help others with the money they raised. Their first proceeds went to the Friendly Home and the Salvation Army. They then also sponsored dog shows, horse shows, art exhibits, lawn parties and summer dances. They soon began to supply funds to other organizations, including the Red Cross, cancer and tuberculosis groups and the Community Chest. In recent years, profits from the Snowball have gone to the West Kentucky Crippled Children Clinic. The Snowball is still a regular event.

For over 50 years, the Charity League has operated its own house at 1921 Broadway, which was deeded to them by one of its members, Mrs. Gus T. Smith. Performing in the Paducah Charity League Follies was one of the most enjoyable experiences it was my good fortune to have. These shows, which were held every other year, gave a lot of local boys and girls opportunities to display their talents and at the same time raise money for handicapped and disabled children. The decade of 1950-1960 was among the best times of my earlier adult days. The family had survived the Depression of the 30s and my service in the military during World War II was over. My brother and two sisters had married and moved far away. After traveling for the Petter Company and being away from home for 4 years, I was happy to be back in the stream of things in Paducah.

I soon became active in community affairs. In 1952, the year I served as chairman of the Second Annual Barbershop show, I was asked to be in the Charity League Follies. Since the show dates were close together, I was uncertain that I would be able to do both. But when my close friends, Henry Ivey and John Wright Polk, insisted, I signed up. That was the beginning of an involvement with the Follies that lasted ten years. I looked forward to the three weeks of activity every other year. Hamming it up and being associated with many Paducahans I knew; some close friends and many merely casual acquaintances, gave me an opportunity to become better friends with many. We always had a good time practicing. Many times I would be in only one skit, or I would be in a group with many others, but I always wanted to be in as many acts as possible, especially performing single roles. All acts were split into practice sessions that varied from an hour, two or three times a week, to almost every night if we would be in many acts. Then after the night sessions, many of us would gather at the home of one or the other and party into the morning hours. We who were single with no family responsibilities could and would attend every night. And some of the married couples also were able to attend and enjoy the fun and companionship. Among the married couples, I particularly remember the Blosses-Bill and Leslie. Leslie, an excellent pianist, accompanied many of the singing and dancing acts. They threw their home open most every night and were willing to "hang out" as long as anyone wanted to stay. They were most gracious hosts.

Three weeks of rehearsals

Rehearsals were held at various places. When the shows were held at the Kentucky Theater, we used the large meeting room on the second floor of the Elks Club, across the street from the theater. For a few years, practice sessions were held upstairs at the Women's Club at 608 Kentucky Avenue. We rehearsed two years in the ballroom on the top floor of Ritz Hotel. It was very comfortable performing in the Follies because we knew most of our fellow performers. Participants were high school age and older. Long-time and newer friends included: June Carneal, Molly Eaton, Beulah Mae Futrell, Sue Hines, Bobby Kennedy, Imogene Igert, Ida Ray Nagel, Bobby Moss, Joanne Polk, Nancy Rice, Betty Sheets, Louise Wahl, Bette Whitlow, Mary Lee Wilmore, Martha Sue Ivey, Charlotte Smith, Josephine Whittemore, Jewell McKnight, Betty Kleckner, Mercer Leroy, Patsy McWaters, Martha Ashcraft, Carolyn Katterjohn, Mary Louis Ezzell, Ella Rena Martin, Mary D. Rieke, Sarah McKinney Smith, Meme Wiley, Betty Hart, Gerry Smith, Ginny Black, Denise (Pug) Sloan, Charlotte Woodall, D. J. Henderson, Gretchen Dallam, Martha Katterjohn, Kate Emery, Margaret Griffin, Evelyn Beyer, Mary Shoup and Mildred Schell.

Shows and Casts

Most of the Follies during the years I participated were staged and directed by Jerome H. Cargill Productions of New York. A director would come to Paducah and set up the acts and select the cast. Each show had a rehearsal pianist, and local orchestras would furnish music. In 1952-53, it was the Frank Webb Orchestra, Jack Staulcup in '55, Charlie James' Ambassadors of Note in '59, and the Hank Weitzel Combo in 1961.The first two shows in '52 and '53, were held at the Kentucky Theater, then shows were at Paducah Tilghman in '55 and '57, at the Kentucky Theater in '59, just before the theater was demolished, and the '61 show was at Tilghman.

Shows I participated in were:

1952

Scene 1- "Strolling thru the Park" - wife—Martha Vaughn, junior— Bernard Ivey, husband—Bill Kressenberg, minister—Barron White
Scene 5- "Odd Moments" - Cissy Davis, Henry Whitlow, Barron White
Scene 2 (Act 2) - "Ah! The Army" -Army officer— Harry Weining, three stupid soldiers—Bill Bloss, Bob Grimm, Barron White, Miss U.S.O.—Theda Bailey

Henry Whitlow, left,
Cissy Davis and Barron
White participate in a
scene for the 1952
Charity League Follies.

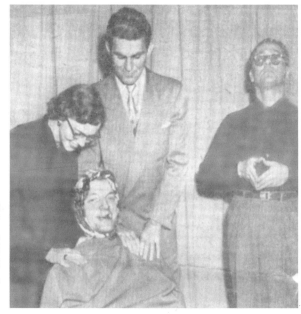

Follies skit
"Preacher and the Brat"
Seated, Barnard Ivey.
Standing, Bill
Kressenberg and
Barron White.

1953 Follies Rehearsal-"There's Nothing Like a Dame"-Left to Right-John W. Polk, Pat Boswell, Phil Wright, D.J. Henderson, Alva Henderson, Barron White, Katherine Eaton, Ed Cave, Doris Wiley, Bertha Wheeler, Bill Bloss, Leslie Bloss at piano.

Charity Singers-Members of the mixed chorus were among local talent starring in the Charity League Follies at Paducah, Kentucky. Members are left to right-Barron White, Neville Stone, George Wiley, John Polk, Jr., Mrs. T.C. Ezell, Nancy Rice, Mrs. E.J. Paxton, Jr., Mrs. Douglas Edwards, Mrs. James Briggs, Mrs. Jesse Carneal, Jr., and Antonette Palmer.

Solos were performed by Joann East and Doris Wiley, sopranos; Barron White, baritone; and David Locke, tenor.

Charity club members, husbands and friends were members of the cast.

1953

Act 1, Scene 1- "Men About Town" - Musco Martin, David Hannan, George Wiley, Weaks Smith, Jack Weldon, George Widener, Burton Robbins, James Hester, John Hester, Cliff Henderson, David Locke, Jack Keiler, Jesse Carneal, Barron White, Bernard Ivey, Bill Bloss, John Polk, Lee Russell, Gene Katterjohn, Jim McCandless, Don McClure, Louis Igert Jr., Bill Wilmore, Bob Davis, Dalton Woodall, Robert Lynn, Phil Wright, Earl Shoup, Norman Sullivan and Paul Murray.
Scene 3- "People Will Say" - Judy Woodall and Barron White
Scene 4- "Nothin' Like 'Em" - sailors—John Polk, Bill Bloss, Ed Cave Jr., Barron White, Jack Keiler, Phil Wright, Cleopatra—Bertha Wenzel, Catherine the Great—D.J. Henderson, Helen of Troy—Doris Wiley, Josephine Bonaparte— Pat Boswell, Mary of Scotland— Katchie Eaton, Mae West— Alva Henderson.
Act 2, Scene 3- "The Cutting Out Party" - the patient—Barron White, doctor—Paul Murray, the photographer—Bill Wilmore, Nurse Jones—Margaret Griffin, the orderly—Bernard Ivey, Dr. Trent—Jim Ryan, stretcher bearers—James Hester, John Hester, the guests—Mary Lee Wilmore, Bill Williams, Bill Bloss, Sue Curtis, Imogene Igert.
Act 2, Scene 4- "Two Hearts" - sung by Barron White and Ruth Lisso, danced by Dalton Woodall, John Polk, Jim McCandless, James Ashcraft, Joe Saxon, John McKnight, Jack Volkamer, Charlotte Woodall, Jewell McKnight, Bobby Houston, Joanne Polk, Katchie Eaton, June Volkamer, Pug Sloan.

1955

Scene 9 - "Look Who's Dancing" -dancing dolls—Toni Palmer, Mary Louise Ezell, Evelyn Paxton, Elizabeth Edwards, Nancy Rice, Marie McClure, Pat Briggs, June Carneal, dancing guys—Tom Ezell, Bernie Behrends, Barron White, Mahlon Shelbourne, Bill Bloss, Neville Stone, Ralph Emery, George Wiley.

1957

Act 1- "Let's Go! You've Been Waiting!" - the Debonaires—Barron White, George Wiley, Louis Myre, Lester Myers, Donald Farrington Jr., Ben Barr, Brooks Jones, Ralph Jones, Henry Dallam, Irving Bright Jr., Russell Jones, Sydney Lester, George Palmer, Bill Shields, Carroll Stewart, David Locke, Ben Bradford, Max Ladt, Wally Reed, Mike Sermersheim, Wyn Stryker, Henry Whitlow, and Jim Brockenborough. The show girls—Pat Kneer, Lucinda Janis, Lynn Davenport, Libby Smith, Jane Bright, Rosemary Dudley, Rosemary Cook, Ginny Black, Betty Kleckner, Gretchen Dallam, Betty Lester, and Nancy Rice. The Rockettes—Nellie Taylor, Nancy Morgan, Judy Holland, Shelbie Burton, Judy Rowland, Betty Delbridge, Dorothy McClure, Ellen Morgan, Lucinda Woodall, Barbara Gunn, Judy Griffin, Vickie Rust, Kathy Taylor, Doris Rothwell, Donna Kay Green, and Judy Stivers.
Act 2- "Gallagher and Shean!" - David Locke and Barron White.
Act 5- "Balling the Jack" - Joan Baker, with Sydney Lester, Donald Farrington Jr., Ralph Jones, Irving Bright Jr., Barron White, Russell Jones, Louis Myre and Brooks Jones.
Act 7- "The Finale" -Helen Karpetas and the entire company.

OCCASIONALLY,
AND FOR NO GOOD REASON AT ALL,

YOU HAVE SEEN LORETTA LIVINGSTON AND JOYCE WILLIAMS, ALSO CISSIE DAVIS, BARRON WHITE AND HENRY WHITLOW.

1959

Scene 5- "At Home with Mother and Dad" - (I remember it well) - Mother—Doris Wiley, Dad—Barron White.

Act 2, Scene 1- "Club Manhattan" - the singing sailors—David Locke, Carroll Stewart, Ron Queen, Barron White, the cop—Ed Cave, Jr., Lulu—Ann Mitchell, gangsters—Norman Sullivan, Harry Johnson, milkman—Tom Yockey, nurse—Peggy Paxton, girls— Betty Ladt, Ginny Black, tramp—John Hester, little girls—Greta Woodall, Frances Bronstein, little boys—Ron Davis, Don Davis, mother— Betty Pettit, the troubadour—Barron White, The Copa Cuties—Sue Bard, Lois Hammond, Barbara Sanders, Joe Boeckman, Clara Harris, Jeanette Watt, Lou Chittenden,

Act 3- "The Back Bay Bistro" - Lizzie Borden—Barbara Sanders, the reporter—Barron White, the district attorney—Bill Bloss, the judge—Francois Pingon, the townspeople—Pat Bradley, Jean Locke, Jackie Truitt, Norman Sullivan, Pat Kneer, Laura Serten, Carolyn Sowell, John Hester, Harry Johnson, Frank Truitt, George Sullivan, Tom Yockey.

Act 6- "Club Orientale"- Teenie Weenie Genie—Kate Emery, the slaves—Barron White, John Barker, the dragon—Betty Ladt, Betty Pettit, Ginny Black, the harem—Joan Lack, Sue Curtis, Mary Doorley, Rosemary Cook, Carolyn Katterjohn, Ruby Myre, Donna Mills, Wanda Edwards.

Act 10- "The Showboat Club" - the interlocutor—Carl Sarten, Tops in Taps—Barbara Williams, Minstrel Maids—Pat Bradley, Pat Kneer, Jean Locke, Mary Barbor, Barbara Sanders, Jackie Truitt, Minstrel Men—Barron White, Jack Harris, David Barbor, David Locke, Frank Truitt, Frank Overmeer.

The finale was a "Farewell to the Kentucky Theater" - A footnote: "Tonight as the curtain closes on the finale of the 1959 Follies, an era in the history of this Paducah theater is also drawn to an end. Our thanks to the Keilers and the Kentucky Theater for adding this charm for 50 years in Paducah's life."

1961

Act 1- "Paris" - Rockettes—Carol Farrington, Sissy Jermstead, Peggie Paxton, Ede Hardy, Barbaranelle Shelton, Gretchen Dallam, Joyce Gholson, Polly Usher, Ray Ann Peel, Ann Ragland, Connie Campbell, Dinny McAllister, Champagne Man—David Locke, Paris girl—Connie Schmidt, Apache—Joyce and Bill LaRue, Paradise man—Barron White.

So ended my involvement with the Follies. The demands of business and the arrival of children changed my priorities, but did not change my enjoyment of later shows. Today, over 40 years later, the league continues to have great shows and do so much to assist the charities that they support.

GEORGE ROCK, 1835-1905

George Rock was born in Hesse Damsstadt, Germany, on January 2, 1835, the second of three children of John and Barbara Rock. His father died in 1848 and the next year his mother brought the three children to America. They settled in Cleveland, Ohio, where Mr. Rock served his apprenticeship at the shoemaker's trade. After learning the trade, he moved to Louisville, Kentucky, where he worked as a journeyman until 1857. In 1856 he married Catherine Seigel, who died in Paducah in 1895. In 1857, he lived in Lafayette, Christian County, Kentucky, and in 1858, he came to Paducah and began the manufacture of custom boots and shoes.

Within a short time, he had a large number of employees. From a small shoemaker's shop in the upper story of a building at Third and Kentucky Avenue, which at that time was the drugstore of John Bonds, Rock moved to "lower" Broadway, at 213 Broadway, between Second and Third streets. He remained at that location until his business grew and caused him to build the handsome three-story building at 321 Broadway. Later he said, "I changed locations four times, but was never off Broadway, and I am within two blocks of any or all of my former locations." In a few years, he branched into the wholesale business and had a number of salesmen who traveled a wide area in the smaller towns and country dealers. In 1897, his son, John became manager-partner of the business. He bought out his father's interest in 1904 and sold the retail business to Koger and Bringhurst, who continued under the George Rock company name.

George Rock had other large interests here. He was vice president of the Paducah Furniture Company and a large stockholder and director of the American-German National Bank. He was one of the promoters in the Pioneer Building and Loan Company, and had large investments in business and residential property. He was a big stockholder in the Paducah Water Company, The Paducah Cordage Company, and the West End Improvement Company. He was also a stockholder in the Mayfield water and light plant, the Carbondale Coal Company at Carbondale and had an interest in a gold mine in Oregon. He was president of the German Evangelical Church at the time of his death.

After a short illness, at the age of 70, he died at his home at Fifth and Monroe, surrounded by his eight children, November 25, 1905. Other survivors were a brother John, and a sister, Mrs. Elizabeth Herman, both of Cleveland. His daughters were Mesdames George Beyer, Henry Beyer, John Bleich, William Katterjohn, Henry Mammen, Jacob Seamon, and Edward Petter.

No minstrel would be complete without end-men, and the Jaycees have them for their annual fall production. Endmen from left to right-Tom Bartholomew, Bill Penry, Frank Nichols, Dick Weir, Jim Temple and Barron White. William Bloss, inter-locutor, is in back of the group.

GEORGE M. ROCK, MINSTREL MAN

I t must have been the late 1920s when I first heard of George M. Rock. He was producing and directing minstrel shows regularly in Paducah. He was always a star performer in them, appearing as a buffoon or a clown. His costume was a red wig, outlandish shirt, calf-length baggy pants with suspenders, red socks and oversize shoes and he had two of his front teeth blackened. His act would include a song or joke, and then he'd grab a curtain on one side of the stage, cock one leg behind him and make several loud guffaws. He produced a number of shows at the Orpheum Theater, located near the southeast corner of North Fifth Street, opposite the old Elks Club.

Some of his earlier minstrels were staged by the Paducah Police and Fire departments. He obtained sponsors from many of the local service clubs and filled the auditoriums of public schools, where the shows would be held. The entire proceeds from most of these shows were given to local charities. Talent for these shows was selected from the sponsors. Usually he would include one or more of his seasoned well-known performers, one of whom was Hubert Bell, a crowd pleaser and long-time employee of Michael Hardware Company. Rock would feature well-known vocal quartets and every performance would have at least two end men in blackface. The format was a series of old-time songs with featured soloists spaced between old corny jokes. It was said that George Rock had no peer as an interlocutor and had a gift for instilling a rollicking fast-moving tempo into his minstrels. I enjoyed participating in several of his shows, as a soloist and once in blackface. One was at the George Rogers Clark School and the other was at Paducah Tilghman.

George Rock died about the time that all public schools were integrated, which had the effect of bringing the traditional minstrel show to an end. But the memory of these old great shows lives on in the minds of old-timers who still recall the "good old days."

George Rock's grandfather, George, started their first business in Paducah in 1835. George Rock was not only known for his minstrels, which he produced throughout western Kentucky, Illinois, Missouri, and Tennessee, but for his outstanding civic work. He was a life-long member of the Unity United Church of Christ, served on the board and was financial secretary for years. His community service included outstanding work in the Benevolent and Protective Order of Elks, of which he was a member for 48 years. He was a member of the Lions Club for 40 years and served as secretary for 10 years. He served on the Kentucky Board Veteran's Committee and administered the program monthly for more than 20 years. A *Paducah Sun-Democrat* reporter wrote of him, "George entertains for the fun of it, but suspects he is motivated by something deeper and more important. Few are the persons who have given as much of their personal time and means for the happiness of others."

SPEAKING OF MINSTRELS

The Paducah Junior Chamber of Commerce, generally known as the Jaycees, presented two minstrels in the 1950s. I became a member in 1935 after I qualified by becoming 21. One could retain his membership until the age of 35, at which time it was assumed he would become affiliated with the Senior Chamber. By the time the first minstrel was given, I had been out of the group for four years, but was asked to participate in the minstrel. In November 1953, the Jaycees presented a John B. Rogers production, "A Shot in the Dark," in the Tilghman High School auditorium. Irvin Hunt, club president and Curtis Vaughn, general show chairman, wrote, "We are indeed grateful for the very generous contribution of talent, time and money which have been given so generously to this production. To all of those Jaycees, civic-minded individuals and friends who participated, we owe a big Thanks."

Jack Staulcup and his orchestra furnished music. Leslie Bloss was pianist. The first three scenes in the first act featured Bill and Leslie Bloss performing "The Taxpayer's Lament," "For the Classical Taste," and "I've Had An Offer of Chinchilla" or "I Don't Like No Cheap Man," backed up by Sue Bard, Pat Briggs, Joy Holston, Jo Anne Jones, Mrs. Thomas Pace, Jo Ashmidt, Mary Ann Saffer, Dorothy Simmons, Mrs. J.B. Temple, Ruth Whitaker, Betty White, and Peggy Fondaw.

"Following the Summer Sun Around," in Scene Four featured Barron White as the tourist, with the "Sunkist" maids— Frances Browning, Peggy Goguem, Joan Helm, Donna Karnes, Martha King and Bobbie Morris. Scene Five, "The Crazy Horsepistol," featured Joan Helm as the nurse, Bob Jones as the patient, Frank Bunch as the doctor, and "assorted" characters. Judy Woodall and Jerry Jennings were the "lovers" in Scene Six, "You Beautiful Son of a Gun," and Phyllis Walden, Barbara Tucker, Patsy Jones, Judy Lee Crutchfield, Louise Jennings, Phyllis Taylor, Peggy Fonda, Hazel Hayes, Susan Bradley, Corrine Burch, Regina Alderson, Patt Rose and Ann Marshall were the "Li'l Cupids."

In Scene Seven, "Down the Swami River, the "Swami" was George White, and "Friend" was B.L. Oss (Bill Bloss). "Eenie, Meenie, Minie and Flo," in Scene Eight was performed by members of the Jaycee Chamber Brigade and Scene Nine featured Hazel Hayes as (Ray) Bolger. Singer Evelyn Beyer and dancer Jo Schmidt were featured in Scene Ten, "Birth of the Blues," with the chorus— Marion Conroy, Joan Helm, Joyce Holston, Jo Anne Jones, Nancy Roach, Mary Ann Saffer, Betty Temple, Ruth Whitaker, Betty White, Mrs. Thomas Pace, Dorothy Simmons and Sue Bard.

Act 2 opened with "Tip Top Merry Minstrel," featuring Interlocutor Bill Bloss and End Men—Sam Bolding, Peter Conroy, Frank Nichols, Bill Penry, Dr. J.B. Temple and Barron White. Musical selections were performed by: the ensemble, Sam Bolding, Mrs. Paul Abell, Frank Nichols, Frank Bunch, Jim Temple, George White, Ann Solomon, Curtis Vaughn, Barron White, Evelyn Beyer, Pete Conroy, Phyllis Taylor and Bill Penry.

BARBERSHOPPING

When World War II was over I returned to work for my former employer, the Petter Supply Company. I was given a job of traveling in Kentucky, Tennessee, Illinois and Missouri, and in 1949, I was asked to come back into the office and take over a department. Although selling on the road was interesting and challenging, being away from home five days a week was getting tiresome and I was happy to be back to regular hours and more free evenings in Paducah. I was 35 and single and wanted to get involved in local activities

When I read in the *Sun-Democrat* that a local chapter of the Society for the Preservation and Encouragement of Barbershop Quartet Singing in America was being formed, I hastened to join, for I had learned to enjoy close harmony. Music has always been a love of mine. From age six until ten, weekly piano lessons were on my schedule. It was only when neighborhood boys said playing the piano was for sissies, that I was shamed into quitting - something I have regretted since. Glee club in high school and later singing with local choral groups was most enjoyable and gave me an opportunity to become involved in plays and shows.

The chapter began with fourteen men and grew to over fifty dyed-in-the-wool barbershoppers. The first show in 1950 at the Tilghman High School Auditorium was a big success, with ten quartets, the thirty-man Paducah chorus and the sixty-man Louisville chorus. Dr. Earl Stivers was the first chapter president, Leo

Osgatharp, the first director and Adrian H. Terrell was general show chairman. Paducah quartets were the Gay Nineties Four, with Stanley Stivers, tenor; George Prince, lead; Earl Stivers, baritone; and Adrian Terrell, bass. The other Paducah quartet, called The Ramblers, was comprised of Carl Howard, tenor; Arvin Bunger, lead; Robert E. Kersey, baritone; and N.O. Story, bass.

The second show was held in 1952, also at Tilghman. The program listed Bob Sanderson, president and director and Barron White, vice president and general chairman. The Paducah Chorus of thirty male voices performed the opening and closing numbers, with quartets from Birmingham, Frankfort, Evansville, Terre Haute

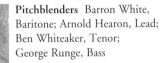

Pitchblenders Barron White, Baritone; Arnold Hearon, Lead; Ben Whiteaker, Tenor; George Runge, Bass

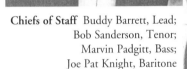

Chiefs of Staff Buddy Barrett, Lead; Bob Sanderson, Tenor; Marvin Padgitt, Bass; Joe Pat Knight, Baritone

The Gay Nineties George Prince, Lead; Stanley Stivers, Tenor; Earl Stivers, Baritone; Adrian Terrell, Bass

The Ramblers Robert E. Kersey, Baritone; Carl Howard, Tenor (back row); Arvin Bunger, Lead; N.O. Story, Bass (far right)

and Paducah in between. Quartets included the Chiefs of Staff, with Bob Sanderson, tenor; Buddy Barrett, lead; Marvin Padgitt, baritone; and Joe Pat Knight, bass. And there were the Pitchblenders, with Ben Whiteaker, tenor; Arnold Hearon, lead; Barron White, baritone; and George Runge Jr., bass. A female quartet, The Four Jays, from Frankfort, also performed. A large and responsive crowd gave the performers in both shows generous and enthusiastic rounds of applause after each number. The Afterglow, a traditional ritual after each barbershop show, was held on the top floor in the dining room of the Ritz Hotel. A room full of dedicated barbershop followers kept the impromptu singing going well into the night.

The chapter held its first meetings at the Immanuel Baptist Church, and then switched to a more convenient place in the private dining room on the first floor of the Ritz Hotel. For many Mondays we used the Ritz top floor dining room. For several years we met at night in the clubroom at the original Paxton Park Pro Shop. Singing with the business and professional men in the Barbershoppers was a most enjoyable and richly rewarding avocation for me.

Members of the chorus were: Fred B. Ashton, Nix Allbritten, Dr. William Blair, Arvin Bunger, Hubert Bell, Buddy Barrett, W.L. Bruce, Sam Bolding, Bill Cooper, Joseph Coulter, Lance Dossett, Frank Dunlap, J.D. Ford and Sid Fulton.

Also Richard S. Gregory, Arnold Hearon, Marvin Hodges, Claude Hinman, Eugene Katterjohn Sr. Kenneth Katterjohn, Emmett Knight, Joe Pat Knight, Robert Kersey, George Long, James E. Moore, Houston McNutt, Allen A. Mossler, R.J. O'Donnell, George Prince, Marvin Padgett, John Bob Padgett, Don Pepper and George Rock.

And John P. Reed, Henry Shapiro, Earl Stivers, Stanley Stivers, Bob Sanderson, N.O. Story, Ed Smith, George Thomas, Ward Thomas, Adrian Terrell, Ed Trevathan, Jack Terrell, Barron White, Lonnie Williams, Gip Watkins and Robert O. Young.

AUGUSTA TILGHMAN HIGH SCHOOL CLASS OF 1931 50TH ANNIVERSARY

Our high school class of 1931 was the last to have an annual. The present Tilghman Library has on file annuals to date from the early 1900s to 1931. A small percentage of the graduating classes have published reunion books, and a few are on file in the history section of the McCracken County Public Library. Our class published books for its 50th and 55th reunions. It is unfortunate that more classes did not do so, as school records are valuable sources of information for researching former students. A complete file on each year would save a tremendous amount of time for researchers.

Paducah native Bill Powell, who was working for the *Louisville Courier-Journal* in 1981, wrote an article on our first reunion. Here are excerpts from his column: "The class, the way I counted pictures in the 1931 year book *The Owaissa*, had 106 members. Sad to say, 34 are known to be deceased. Some of the ones who are dead were friends I made in the newspaper business. They include George Jacobs, who was mayor of Paducah in the 1950s; Warren Eaton, who became Circuit Court Judge of McCracken County; Murray Rogers, who used to run a weekly paper here and was always needling city officials and the *Paducah Sun-Democrat*; Edwin Gunter, whom I met in 1933 when, as a vacationing student from Murray State where he played football, he came to pick strawberries for Chris Edmonds of Symsonia; and Adelaide Eubanks, who died with her husband, Dr. Hal Houston, after the fire that struck their home in Murray."

The Owaissa that year was an interesting book that would cost a fortune to publish now. The yearbook was dedicated to Walter C. Jetton, who was only in his eighth year of a 35-year career as Tilghman principal. The class prophecy was written by Burgess Scott, who worked on *Yank Magazine* in World War II, and now lives in Michigan and is a staff writer for the *Ford Times*. Burgess's predictions were amusing, but few came true. He correctly forecast that Howard Moss and Mildred Lloyd would be man and wife. The tramp he predicted would be Paul Twitchell. Paul did lead a strange life, becoming the head of some kind of religious group.

The reunion committee was headed by Bill Feiler and was composed of Herman Graham, Roberta Gregston Heath, Barron White, Norman Scott, Walter Cartee, Dorothy Weimann, Ruth Rogers Decker, Elsie Mae Jeffords Neistrath, Bob Hassman, Jimmy Yeltema and Bill Mills. Master of ceremonies and booklet producer was Barron White. The reunion was held at the Paducah Country Club with entertainment provided by Donn Wisdom, minister of music at the First Baptist Church.

Welcoming remarks included the following; "Reading all the cards and letters has made me realize what a great class we had. Having graduated in the midst of the Depression of the early thirties, living and surviving through the great flood of 1937, through three wars, the social and moral depression of the sixties, and accomplishing all that we have, makes me realize we made a great contribution to society and to the productive output of our country. Our class quickly permeated every segment of activity in the country, performing their chosen tasks quietly, with dignity and energy, without fanfare or notoriety. I feel we made a big contribution in helping our great country show the greatest advancement ever in technology and achievement. We lived through and are still enjoying the greatest years ever in our country's history. No other period of time can begin to match the tremendous strides made during our lifetime in whatever field you care to check - be it science, medicine, athletics, communications, electronics, space - what have you. Our class contributed artists and accountants, bookkeepers and sellers, coaches and consultants, doctors, druggists, nurses, housewives and hospital workers, farmers and pharmacists, ministers and musicians, lawyers and librarians, superintendents, salesmen, publishers, and newsmen, and the list goes on - people in all walks of life, each making his own contribution to active and productive accomplishment."

A recent recap of the class showed that 47 members lived in

Kentucky, with 38 of those remaining in Paducah. Five lived in Florida, seven in Tennessee, six in California, three in Arizona, two each in Ohio, Mississippi and New Jersey and one each in Georgia, Louisiana, Michigan, Illinois, New York, North Carolina, Indiana, New Hampshire, and Pennsylvania.

AUGUSTA TILGHMAN HIGH SCHOOL CLASS OF 1931 55TH REUNION, 1931-1986

The 55th reunion of the ATHS Class of 1931 was held on September 18, 1986, at the Holiday Inn on Joe Clifton Drive. Thirty-six members, eight spouses included, made reservations. All either lived in Paducah or less than hour away. A booklet was given out to all, containing the 31 letters that had been received in response to a request mailed out early in the year for members to write of their activities since the 50th reunion. These letters were bound with the same front cover as the 50th, except the words "PLUS FIVE" had been added. Another addition was a list of names of those who had died since 1981.

The meeting was just an informal noon get-together, with no program or entertainment. The 50th reunion emcee chaired the affair, which included a moment of silence and a prayer for the twelve members who had died since the 50th meeting. We were there about two hours, with the last hour for goodbyes. We realized that this was likely to be our last meeting, which gave all a feeling of sadness and finality. Those who attended were: Norman and Doris Scott, Mary Elizabeth Boyd, Catherine Moore, Mr. and Mrs. Herman Graham, Eloise Cox, Dorothy Weimann, Mary Alice Carneal, Elizabeth Dixon, Bob and Loraine Emerson, Elizabeth Craig Murphy, Sue and Haywood Stephenson, Bill Feiler, Mabel Reed, Ullonda Hannin, Mildred Ross White and spouse, Mercer Leroy, Walker Turner, Virginia Dallas, Mr. and Mrs. James Clark,

200

MY PADUCAH

Opal Shelton, Jeane Wallerstein Shapiro, Barron and Zelma White, Katie Hart, Morris McBride and Beatrice Yeltema.

During the period between our 50th and 55th class reunions, the members who died were: Howard Moss-probation officer; Mildred Moss-deputy county clerk; William Mills-sales, National Cash Register; Burgess Scott-*Yank Magazine*-WWII-technical editor-*Ford Times*; Jimmie Yeltema-floral designer, Cherry Florist; John Galloway-stock keeper, ICRR; Clarence Cox-attorney; Bob Hassman-food broker; Walter Cartee-letter carrier; Jack Dulsworth-farmer; Joe Wilson-tax attorney; and Woodrow "Woody" Wilson-hotel, restaurant business.

Since 1986, others who have passed away are: Mary Elizabeth Boyd-court stenographer; Custis Fletcher-Episcopal rector; Herman Graham-representative, Kentucky Department of Revenue; Pauline Callis Newman-printer/artist; Opal Shelton-Bureau of Health; and Sue Griffith Stephenson-secretary.

As of July 2001, I know of two others still living in Paducah and two living out of state. They are:

* William (Bill) Feiler, a retired pharmacist, who with his wife Mary Frances Dunn Feiler, also a pharmacist, owned and operated Dunn Drug Store. Mary Frances died in 1997, after 57 years together. Their four sons are: Dr. William A. Feiler Jr., Los Angeles, California; Lt. Colonel John P. "Jack" Feiler, San Antonio, Texas; Fred and Matt Feiler, Paducah. Bill and I attend Rotary every Wednesday noon and enjoy golf together at Paxton Golf Course.

*Jeanne Wallerstein Shapiro, former owner of Jean's women's store, who was married to Henry Shapiro. They had one son and one daughter and two grandchildren. Their son Bob Shapiro, who operated Jean's for a number of years, is an avid outdoorsman and is presently promoting the Maiden Alley Theater, now open in the former Petter Supply building.

* Elizabeth Dixon, who was a secretary at Claussner Hosiery Mills for years, moved to Hickory, North Carolina, when Claussner

opened the Marvel Specialty Company there. She now lives in the Lakeshore Villa Mobile Home Retirement Community, about four miles from the city limits of Tampa, Florida. She keeps busy doing volunteer work at a hospital, attends exercise classes regularly, teaches Sunday school at the Baptist church and enjoys reading and the activities at the village.

* Mary Frances Williams Ballowe, who moved to Sun City, Arizona, after her husband George R. Ballowe retired from the U.S. Treasury Department in Washington, D.C.

408 WASHINGTON STREET PADUCAH

I received a letter on July 17, 1999 from Melissa Morgan of Paducah, who wrote, "In 1916-17, my grandfather Harville Martin lived in a boarding house while working at South Central Bell. As the boarding house is no longer standing at 408 Washington Street, my dad and I are interested in learning about the house, as well as possibly coming across a picture or two, if such exists. If you are aware of this boarding house and know anything about it, I would appreciate your letting me know."

I knew that the house at that address and all the houses in that block were demolished years ago (around 1965) when the new Paducah City Hall was built. Since I lived in the 500 block on Washington (in the Napoleon Apartments) when my family moved to Paducah in 1923, I was familiar with houses in the neighborhood, but didn't remember that particular house. The only one I recall in that block was Dorian's private school, two doors west of 408.

There were several boarding houses in the downtown at that time. The very next day after receiving that letter, I was doing volunteer work for the Paducah Ambassadors, helping passengers on the riverboat docked at the foot of Broadway. Two other Ambassadors, Katherine and Hank Batts, were also there, and while we were sitting in the boat's dining room, waiting for the gangplank to be re-positioned, I told Hank about the inquiry. Hank said, "I know that old house...in fact, Steve Etter lived there, and the house became the location for a mission for the First Baptist Church." He also told me that he knew a man who lived there for several years and he gave me the man's name and suggested that I phone him.

So I could hardly wait to get home and give him a call. I called the man, Hadred L. Brown, who lives on Monroe. He said he remembered living there and that he had a small snapshot of the home that he would let me copy. The next morning, I went by and had a delightful talk with H.L. "Butch" Brown and his wife Imogene. She said she knew me, and I recognized him as a man who had worked downtown for years. He said he had been a watchmaker at M. Manus Jewelry for years. Butch said he lived upstairs in the house with the Etters during the flood and was stranded when the water got too high for him to get his car out of the garage to high ground. He said they cleaned the bathtub thoroughly, and then while they still had water, they filled it to the top and used it for drinking and cooking all during their stay. When they needed water to flush the toilet, they would walk down the stairs with a bucket, to the floodwaters that came halfway up the steps and use it for flushing. When they finally were evacuated, they stepped out of the kitchen window onto the top of the garage and climbed into the boat that took them out to high ground.

Butch also told me that while he lived there, Steve Etter and his mother decided to live out in the country, so they built a house and moved away from 408. After a few years, when Steve had moved from his mother's house, his mother became lonesome living by herself and tried to get the Washington Street house back, but the Mueniers, who had been there when they were, refused to sell them the house.

In my chat with the Browns, Mrs. Brown told me that a cousin of hers named Lawrence Lucas had worked for Petter years ago and told me a few tales about him. I knew Lucas well in those early years when I first worked at Petter Supply and had, in fact, traveled with him one week. I kept in touch with him for many years until I went to the Army. Strangely enough, I have been writing stories about my experiences at Petter and had tried to write about Lucas, but found only a meager amount of information.

The point of this whole story is that are countless numbers of people right here in Paducah living among us, who have histories all their own that would be fascinating, if we could bring them to light and record them. Many have boxes and boxes of snapshots and newspaper clippings that are treasures of old Paducah history. This story is but one small example.

MEMBER OF THE PADUCAH JAYCEES

Dick Fairhurst moved to Paducah in 1928 and organized the Paducah Jaycees, the first Jaycee club in Kentucky. He was elected president. Ward Thomas was vice president. They received a national charter in 1929. Eleven men were the first members. Those I knew were: Russell Thomas, Ward's older brother; Jack House, Adrian Terrell, Claude Baker, Bill Paxton, Prewitt Lackey and Buck Burnett.

When I joined in 1935, there were approximately 75 members. Meetings were held every Monday at 7 p.m. on the second floor of the Masonic Hall at Fifth Street and Kentucky Avenue. Later we met at the Irvin Cobb Hotel. One of the first projects we had in 1935 was the first Turtle Derby, a good money raiser, held at Hook's Park. After the 1937 flood, the Jaycees erected a marker for the statue of Chief Paduke, which had been moved from in front of the old post office to a grass plot at 19th and Jefferson streets. The biggest and best-known project that included all members was the building of Paxton Park Municipal Golf Course. Newspaper editor and publisher Edwin J. Paxton was the power behind the throne, as he supported Jaycee Sam Livingston, who spearheaded a fund drive to pay for the 101-acre plot at the intersection of Jackson Street and Lone Oak Road. Buck Burnett was chairman, Henry Whitlow, treasurer. The original golf commission was comprised of Sam

Livingston and Edwin J Paxton, Sr. When Burnett moved to Memphis, Dick Fairhurst took his place. The course opened July 18, 1940, with Mr. Paxton hitting out the first ball. Marion Miley, a lady professional golfer from Lexington, Kentucky, and Brooks Starr, Paxton Park's first golf pro, were the main attractions.

The 15 years that I was a member was a very enjoyable and rewarding experience. Many of my friends, before and during my time, were members and have been lifetime friends. Those that I recall include: Paul Abell, Lawrence Allbritton, W L. Beasley, Arvin Bunger, Bob Cherry, Russ Chittenden, Jack Clark, Jim Curtis, J. C. Dudley, Bill Ezzell, Ed Hank, Ed Hulett, Bob Hulsey, Henry Ivey, Lee Livingston, Joe Glover, Earl Logan, Bob Morrow, Frank Paxton, Bill Powell, Richard Ragland, Murray Rogers, Jack Rottgering, Paul Rottgering, Bob Thomas, Charles "Chubby" Wahl, Henry Whitlow, Earl Seay, Bob Hassman, Eugene Katterjohn, Sam Livingston, Pelham McMurry, and Dick Fairhurst.

PADUCAH-MAYFIELD

Back in the 1930s there was not only an intense rivalry between the Mayfield and Paducah high schools, but also between the Paducah boys dating Mayfield girls and Mayfield boys dating Paducah girls. But as I remember, it was a very friendly rivalry and no blood was spilled over the situation. Mayfield was able to attract large crowds to the big bands, which were booked frequently at the American Legion Hall. Couples would come from all over western Kentucky. And many of us who could not afford dates, would show up to meet and dance with the girls who came. Those were the days of "break" dances and we stags could circulate among the couples and dance with every girl we chose. There were no tables and few chairs-everyone came to dance or just congregate around the bandstand and listen to the music. All the big name bands played there at one time or other. After the first few visits, we began to eagerly await the next one so we could be with and dance with all the girls.

As I recall, most of the tickets cost less than five dollars a couple and about half for stags. As you entered the door with your ticket in hand, the attendant would snap a distinctive colored tag to your lapel, which was your pass in and out of the hall at intermission, or if you needed to get in and out. After every performance, many of us would save our tags, by snipping them from the under side with the hope that the same tag would be used, but that seldom happened.

On some occasions a carful of us would go over even though we did not have enough money to buy a ticket for each. We would buy two tickets, flip a coin to see which two could go in first, then in a while they would come out, give their tags to two, who could go in and stay until intermission. Those outside would wait in the car for their turn. Sometimes we would sneak in those who could not afford a ticket. One with a date would go in, remove his tag, loan it to a friend long enough to get the one inside and get his tag back. Anyone dancing without a ticket would not be challenged unless he tried to go out and return. After intermission, the doorkeeper would relax his vigilance and if a non-ticket holder had not been able to manage to get in, it was no trouble. You would just walk in with someone with a ticket.

After a few dances, we began to know the girls in Mayfield, Murray, Fulton, Hickman, Bardwell and Barlow. Some Paducah boys who were not going steady and were lucky enough to have access to cars would date some of the area girls on weekends between dances.

PADUCAH MURAL
IN THE FEDERAL BUILDING

It is probably a pretty safe bet that fewer than 50 percent of the people presently living in Paducah know of or have seen the 72-foot-long mural hanging in the foyer of the Federal Building at 501 Broadway. The mural, which depicts the colorful early history of Paducah, was painted by fourteen amateur artists on twelve light-weight 4-by-6-foot wooden panels, over a twelve-month period, starting in 1960. The project required 5,000 man-hours and 100 dozen eggs, used in the painting mixture. It was found that a mixture of ground colors and the yolks from fresh country eggs was better than oil. The mural shows this western Kentucky river town in the early Indian and log cabin days, when steamboats plied the rivers, and during the early days of our railroads. Many months of research went into the project. Many authorities and books on Paducah history were reviewed to make the result authentic.

Most of the work was done in the basement of Bess Locke, 3434 Buckner Lane. Bess was the wife of Sam M. Locke, assistant manager of the Petter Supply Company, where I was employed. Bess was an excellent amateur artist and was one of the fourteen mural painters. They all worked through the fall and early winter of 1960 and through the spring, summer and into the next fall, until it was completed. Ray Black and Sons installed the paintings. The finished product was offered to the federal government as a gift and was accepted by the General Services Administration, with offices in Chicago, Illinois.

None of the artists who participated were named when the story was released, as they wanted the painting to be identified as a community effort. Since then their names have been published. They were Mary Pat Boswell, Morris Boswell, Dorothy Gaylor, French Helsey, Polly Newman, Bess Locke, Virginia Reed, David Reed, Opal Reid, Beulah Tucker, Virginia Smith, Nancy Paro, Mabel Williams, and the teacher, Admiral Eugene Paro. The murals were numbered right to left, 1 through 12, the way they were installed, because the main entrance was located on the right side of the building. The scenes are:

1.   Before white men, roving Indians camped at the site of Paducah.
2.   Chickasaw Indians, it is believed, were the area's first inhabitants.
3.   Brothers Will and James Pore had started the first cabin

by 1821.
4. In this clearing a settlement - first called Pekin - began to grow.
5. In 1827, William Clark surveyed land left by his brother, George.
6. Clark renamed the settlement Paducah, perhaps for an Indian chief.
7. A railroad, financed locally, began its run to Mayfield in 1859.
8. The *James Campbell* was first of many Paducah-built locomotives.
9. U.S. Grant's men occupied Paducah in 1861, to attack southerners.
10. In high water, Grant's men set out for Fort Henry in February 1862.
11. Paducah by the 1860s, a crossroads of river trade.
12. From 1870 on, for several decades, the steamboat ymbolized progress.

(This information was obtained from newspaper accounts in the *Paducah Sun-Democrat* and the *Courier-Journal.*)

PAXTON PARK GOLF COURSE PROS

BROOKS STARR

B rooks Starr made a lifetime career of golf. He caddied as a boy at the first municipal golf course in Paducah, which was at Annie Baumer Field, adjacent to Bob Noble Park. A native of Paducah, he attended school at Reidland and St. Mary's Academy. He was an excellent golfer and won many trophies in competition in several states. He started playing professionally in 1931. He never missed playing in the Kentucky Open or the Irvin Cobb tournaments. He even played against the legendary great Walter Hagen, in a tournament in Louisville.

He was golf pro at the Old Lakeview Country Club, now

Brooks Starr at U.S. Air Force Base
Smyrna, Tennessee-1942

Rolling Hills, for four years, and then moved to the Princeton Country Club in 1935. From there he was pro at the Mayfield Country Club from 1935 until 1939. He was the first pro for the Edwin J. Paxton Municipal Golf Course, having been hired in 1939, before the official opening in 1940. A large crowd was on hand for the opening ceremony, which featured an exhibition match between Starr and Marion Miley of Lexington, one of the all-time greats of women's golf. *Paducah Sun-Democrat* Editor Edwin J. Paxton, drove out the first ball and a marker was imbedded in the spot where it landed. Paducah Mayor Pierce Lackey smashed a bottle of champagne on the clubhouse and shouted, "I christen thee El Bucko," after "Buck" Burnett, who had been the chief fundraiser and worker of the Jaycees, who were in charge of making the course a reality.

Brooks remained at Paxton until 1942, when he entered the U.S. Air Force. He was assigned to special services and was in charge of the golf course at the Air Force Base at Smyrna, Tennessee, where he was stationed throughout the war. He was discharged in 1945 and returned to Paducah to resume his work as pro at Paxton. For a few years, he operated a sporting goods store at 3rd Street and Kentucky Avenue. In 1949, State Conservation Commissioner Henry Ward, former *Sun-Democrat* editor, selected Starr to supervise construction of the 18-hole golf course at Kentucky Dam Village. Brooks put all his time and energy into this project and took pride in being there to show off his handiwork. Then a change in the state administration occurred in 1954 and he was terminated. He went back to where he had started his professional golf career, at the

Rolling Hills Country Club, until his friends were back in the administration at Frankfort and rehired him as manager of the course at Kentucky Dam in 1960.

His life was shaken by several family tragedies, including the death of his father Ben Starr, who was killed in a freak tornado at the state-owned family home near Kentucky Dam and by the death of his sister's husband in a car wreck. In August of 1960, after a period of despondency and suffering from a nervous condition, Brooks died. He was 54 years old. He was buried in Mt. Kenton Cemetery. He was a member of Reidland Methodist Church.

ANTHONY VINCENT GENOVESE

Vince Genovese's first career was as a musician and band-leader. He began when he was paid to play the guitar at country dances. He took trumpet lessons and played in the Murphysboro, Illinois, high school band, which launched his interest in music. Then from 1934 to 1943, his 10-member band, "Music to Please by Vince Genovese," played throughout the Midwest. His specialty was jazz and the swing music of the 1930s and 1940s. The band was disbanded when he joined the Army Air Force during World War II.

After the war, he found interest in music was changing, so started looking for other work. Since his dance "gigs" were at night, he had been able to play a lot of golf and after playing in some tournaments, he decided to become a pro and became manager of a golf shop in Murphysboro.

Vince came to Paducah in 1951 to be the golf professional at the Edwin J. Paxton Municipal Golf Course. For a few months, before he located a home and could bring his wife, Mary here, he lived in the pro shop at Paxton. He enlarged his stock of golf equipment, and added golf shirts and shoes to his inventory. During his tenure, he promoted the Irvin Cobb Golf Championships into the area's top event. He added a pro-am tournament on the Friday before the 36-hole Cobb on Saturday and Sunday. He also started the Tri-State Seniors Tournament that became an annual event. He said he gave 8,000 lessons during his life as golf pro. In 1964, he was named Kentucky's PGA Pro of the Year.

When I returned from the Air Force and was back living in Paducah in 1949 after having spent four years traveling for Petter Supply, I resumed golfing at Paxton. I played most afternoons after work and on Saturdays. I joined the Paxton Park Players Association and served as treasurer for several years. We worked with Vince and helped him with tournaments and special golf outings. Most of the previous pros at Paxton were more interested in playing golf than running a business, so it was good to have someone in charge who was seriously interesting in promoting golf, the course and helping it grow. Vince was active in the Paducah Night Lions Club and for 15 years served as director and emcee of the Miss Paducah Beauty Pageant. After retiring from Paxton Park, he served as golf pro on a temporary basis at the Rolling Hills Course. He remained active, and was often seen helping golfers with their swing at driving ranges. He and Mary were able to travel, and on one occasion visited Rome, a retirement gift from the Paxton Park Players Association. Vince died May 5,1998 at the age of 89. Mary preceded him in death. Vince's funeral services were held at the St. Thomas More Catholic Church, with burial in the St. Andrew's Cemetery in Murphysboro.

DANIEL "KAYO" MULLEN

Kayo Mullen was born January 3,1936 in Paducah. When I first knew him he was a caddie at Paxton Park Golf Course, as were his brothers, Eddie "Moon" and David "Crawpap." I did not know his older brother, Charles, until after he retired and worked part time as a marshal and starter at Paxton. Nor did I know his younger brother, Larry, until he was grown and playing golf professionally. The Mullen brothers were popular caddies and among the first to be called by the caddie master. I rarely was able to hire one of them, as they would be booked before I got there. Caddies

E.D. "Kayo" Mullen-Golf
Pro, Paxton Park

were able to play free on Monday mornings and most of them became excellent golfers. When I began to play at Paxton after it was opened in 1940, Kayo and others would try to get me to play for 25 cents a hole, but by then they were close to being scratch golfers and I knew better than to bet with them, for I knew I would lose.

Kayo joined the U.S. Marine Corps in 1956 and served at Parris Island, South Carolina, and McAlester, Oklahoma. Before being released from the Marines, he married Velva Richards in Corinth, Mississippi, on January 18,1958. They returned to Paducah, where he resumed his job as assistant golf professional at Paxton. In March 1961, he accepted the position as head golf pro at Poplar Meadows Country Club, Union City, Tennessee. He remained there until 1974 and then returned to Paducah to become golf course superintendent. In 1976, he became golf director, a position he held until retirement two years ago. His son, Danny, who had served as assistant pro, was then selected as his replacement. Danny remains as club pro today.

Kayo ran the course "hands on." He posted rules and procedures for playing and saw that they were enforced. He often clashed with some who felt that their years of being members permitted them to bend the rules. Kayo saw to it that the rental carts were kept in good running condition and was able to have Paul Sargent on hand to make the repairs. As a result of his good work and longtime devotion and loyalty to the course, the road into the park is named Paul Sargent Drive.

Since turning over the reins as pro to Danny, Kayo took over the management of the greens and fairways. He has kept them in tip-top shape through the years and is generally known to be one of the best grass men in the area. The Mullens also have two daughters, Tammy and Tina. All five members of the family are good golfers and play regularly.

OLD LANDMARKS

When you are young and growing up in a town, you are inclined to think the places you knew and the businesses you visited would always remain. But when you look back after a lifetime of living in the same place, you realize that although the changes have been gradual, over the long haul, they have been quite drastic. That is what has happened in Paducah.

For example, the old landmarks I knew and loved that are no longer around include:

• The Wharfboat at the foot of Broadway.
• Mooney' s restaurant on South Second.
• Walker's Drugstore on the southeast corner of Fifth and Broadway.
• Other downtown drugstores on the Broadway corners of Fourth, Fifth and Sixth.
• The downtown movie houses - Arcade, Columbia, Orpheum, Kozy and Star.
• The Palmer House Hotel at Fifth and Broadway.
• The Oxford Hotel at Fifth and Jefferson.
• Temple Israel at Seventh and Broadway.
• The Carnegie Library at Ninth and Broadway.
• Dunbar's Drugstore at Broadway and Fountain Avenue.
• Albritten's Drugstore at 32nd and Broadway.
• The Twinkling Star and the Peacock Garden in the west end.
• Buster Seay's Breeze at Leeder Bottoms, between Paducah and Mayfield.
• Bichon's Inn and Mac & Mac's on Cairo Road.

All of these are now but happy memories.

WHO HOCKED THE CLOCK?

Old records show that Paducah has had three city halls. The city bought a site at 124 North Fourth Street and erected a 2-story red brick building. The lower floor served as a courtroom and the upper room as council chamber and clerk's office. The jail was in the basement.

A new city hall was built in 1883, at a cost of $20,000. This replaced the old Fourth Street city hall. A new clock and bell were purchased by the city. William Nagel of Nagel & Meyer Jewelers was contracted to install the clock for $825. The bell was cast in 1853 by the Troy Bell Foundry Company of Troy, New York, and was installed in the Paducah City Hall in 1883. It rang every hour in the clock tower. Being housed in the clock tower, the bell was seldom seen, except by a few people who climbed above the attic to wind the clock. Nagel had to go there once a week back in the 1950s and 1960s to crank up the weights, which took him about fifteen minutes each time. It was dirty work, with everything covered with pigeon droppings and dust. The third floor was added in 1909 and an elevator and new equipment was installed at a cost of $15,284. This building was in use until the new Edward Durrell Stone City Hall was erected in January 1965 at 300 Washington. It covered a whole city block and cost approximately $150,000. It was dedicated February 28, 1965.

Shortly after the new city hall was completed the old building was demolished. Mayor Tom Wilson and a group of his friends purchased the old clock and bell tower, in order to save it from the wrecking crews razing the old city hall. A caption on a picture showing the clock being lowered says, "GOING, GOING. The old city hall is coming to an end of its 83 years at the corner of 4th and Kentucky." A landmark for years, the old clock above the old city hall came down to be stored away until something could be decided about where to place it. Wilson had the clock securely wrapped in a tarpaulin cover and bound with rope and stored in a six-foot-high wooden platform behind the Noble Park caretaker's residence. It

City Hall clock

remained there for several years.

In August 1966, Walter L. "Dub" Beasley, a lifelong friend and a man interested in preserving Paducah's history, took his two daughters, Jennifer and Meade, to Noble Park to show them the old city hall clock, still securely wrapped and tied with rope and resting on the wooden platform. He pulled back the covering long enough to take a picture. This was probably the last time the clock saw the light of day until a few years later when it mysteriously disappeared. Fortunately, the pre-Civil War phosphor-bronze bell that was removed when the building was razed was saved. "Tom Wilson had it stored in the Terminal Warehouse building for several years," said Beasley, who played a leading role in preserving the bell. A 1983 fire in the warehouse severely damaged the bell, which was retrieved from the ashes in three large pieces. Wilson had the three pieces hauled away for storage at Richard Brown's

Mitchell Machine Shop on South 3rd Street.

About a year later, Beasley heard that a junk dealer was interested in buying what was left of the bell. In the summer of 1986, he offered to store the pieces at his monument yard at 1101 South Thirteenth Street. One Saturday, a motorist lost control of his car on the curve in front of the Beasley business and ran into the bell, breaking it into more pieces. That could have been the end of it, but for the efforts of Mayor Gerry Montgomery, city officials and VMV Enterprises, the railroad company at the old I.C. Shops. In 1990, VMV President Paul Seaton and officials had the pieces taken to their shops. Two skilled craftsmen, Max Norwood and John Millay, using materials donated by Welder's Supply, spent 340 hours welding the pieces together.

The next problem was moving the bell from the shops to city hall. That took about a dozen volunteers from Falconite Crane, Jones Glass, Ironworkers Local 782, along with a crew from Beasley Monument and city workers. A plywood box held the bell safe from harm until the "unboxing" ceremony held Monday September 17,1990. Beasley donated a slab of white marble from Colorado for the base. This was the closest he could find to match the two pedestals already in the foyer. The bell was mounted on the marble perch on October 31,1991.

So, on the 203rd anniversary of the signing to the U.S. Constitution, the 3,500-pound bronze bell that once proudly hung in the clock tower of the old city hall had come home. Mayor Gerry Montgomery and others have searched for the clock, without finding any trace of it. Could it have been sold? It is hard to imagine someone stealing it without being seen loading it and hauling it away. A few of us are still trying to discover some trace of it. We hope that someone will eventually find it. We can't believe anyone would destroy such an historic landmark.

HARAHAN HOBOES

In my first book, *I Remember Paducah When...*, published in November 2000, there is a story about the Harahan Hoboes. Recently, I ran across the only written evidence that such a group ever existed. One of the two letters was written by Harold "Hoppy" Futrell, dated December 19, 1961 and was addressed to "Former Hoboes: Subject: Possible Reunion." The other letter, undated, was headed, "Report to the Hoboes," and written by Roby Robertson.

Hoppy's boyhood home was at 16th and Harrison, one block west of Harahan. He wrote from his residence at 3324 Lone Oak Road, located a short distance south of what was then the center of Lone Oak. In his front yard, facing the highway was his office, a one-room building where he operated a small retail sand and gravel business. The Federal Materials Company on the riverfront would deliver him a truckload and dump it in front of his office. Hoppy sold to area contractors, a few shovels at a time. For those who needed only small quantities, it was easier to get it at his place than to drive all the way to town and back. This suited Hoppy fine and he had a lot of leisure time to read the detective and gun magazines that he enjoyed. Hoppy was single, divorced from Beulah (Beulie) Boyles, and liked his own independent lifestyle.

Hoppy was always fascinated with weapons and in his younger days as operator of Hoppy's Fast Freight Company, loved to ride shotgun with his drivers as they hauled their cargoes of alcoholic beverages from distilleries through dry states. They were hi-jacked on several occasions, and afterwards he would ride in the passenger seat with his loaded shotgun on the ready.

Hoppy served in the Army during World War II and we had a chance meeting in Brussels, Belgium, at the end of hostilities when we were on R&R. He stayed in the reserves and every year afterwards, arranged to be called up to serve on temporary duty, in addition to the obligatory two-week service time. During his last few years, we would see Hoppy now and then, alone at one of the local restaurants. He died in 1989 at age 74.

Roby was formerly a resident of Harahan, two doors from Clay Street. His letter was written from Eaton Avenue, Owensboro, Kentucky, where he and his wife, Helen Cooley Robertson, lived. Helen, incidentally, lived on Harahan also, on the northwest corner of Monroe, when they were dating. They had moved to Bowling Green, Kentucky, where Roby was employed for a number of years by the Lamp Division of General Electric. On one of my business trips to Bowling Green for Petter in the late 1940s, I spent a pleasant evening with them. Later, when the Sylvania Company bought the GE plant, they were moved to the plant at Owensboro, where they were living when Roby died few years ago. At present, Helen still lives there. Their daughter Ann is married to Vic Speck of Paducah, and they have three daughters Suzanne, Sarah, and Carrie. Suzanne was a good friend of our daughter Liz. They were in the same class at Paducah Tilghman. Vic is the owner of Welder's Supply on Bethel Street in the industrial park on the south side. The Speck family for many years operated the Paducah Iron Company on the north side of South First Street, on the bank of the Tennessee River, until the floodwall was built in 1940.

Hoppy's letter was co-signed by Bus Rutter, who lived near the corner of Park Avenue and 16th Street during his school years, and ran around with the Harahan boys. Everyone called him "Bus," although his name was William L. Rutter. He married Mary Ellen Bradshaw, who was Paducah's Strawberry Queen in 1938. They had two children, Tom and Rebecca. When I returned to civilian status after World War II, Bus was a salesman for new cars at Peters Motor Company, the Ford dealer at 1128 Broadway. New cars were hard to get and there was a waiting list. Bus took my order for one, but told me it would be a few months before Peters could get it included in a trailer load. He suggested that if I could arrange to pick it up at the Ford plant in Louisville, it would save three to four week's time. So when I was told it was available, I flew there, picked it up and drove home. Bus was city treasurer of Paducah in the early '60s, when Robert C. Cherry was mayor. Later he was office manager for Kolb Bros. Drug Company. He and Mary Ellen lived on Ridgewood until he died in the 1970s. Mary Ellen is at present living on Jefferson Street.

REFLECTIONS

Having just completed writing book number two, I need to pause and see what has been accomplished and what I should do from now on. Book number one, published in November 2000, has exceeded my fondest expectations, with over 2,000 copies having been purchased.

When I started writing over 25 years ago, after surviving a life-threatening malignancy, I intended to focus on experiences I had while employed by the Petter Supply Company, but this led to exploring the history of Paducah before and beyond my personal knowledge or experience. There is so much rich information of years past that lies buried in the pages of old daily newspapers. Most of us will never know or care about it unless it is preserved in books or publications that beg to be written.

As we have crossed the threshold of a new century it should be worthwhile to assess the last 100 years and wonder what the next 100 have in store for us. Today Paducah has approximately 26,000 residents, the majority being of retirement age. Enrollment in our schools is static and facing some decline. Despite the loss of most of our manufacturing facilities, Paducah seems to be healthy, with a lot of activity in and through the area. Urban sprawl is reaching out all over McCracken County, traffic is heavy, hotels and restaurants are crowded, and service companies are flourishing. The city's image is more attractive than ever, with an encouraging expansion of tourism. With things looking up for the Convention Center, the Quilt Museum, the Performing Arts Center, River Heritage Museum, Seamen's Institute, Tilghman Museum, Whitehaven, Maiden Alley Cinema, Market House Museum and downtown specialty shops and restaurants, Paducah will enjoy an influx of visitors for some time.

I remain puzzled by what engine is fueling our economy. We have to be hurt by the loss of all those factory payrolls of yesteryears. We should be thankful for our rivers, which since day one have been a steady source of income for many of our people. Trade journals cite that the river industry in Paducah is supported by over 200 companies that serve the river trade. This is a constant and continuous impetus that has nowhere to go but up.

So where should my focus be for future writings? The second book leaned toward more emphasis on people than on buildings and business. Thomas Macauley, the greatest of English historians, said, "The history of a country is best told in the record of the lives of its people." This is good advice to follow.

BIBLIOGRAPHY & PHOTO CREDITS

Directories, City of Paducah, 1882 to present
Fairhurst, Richard E. *The Fairhurst Essays: A Public Look
    At a Private Memoir,* The Patric Press, 1980
Johnston, Bob and Jack, Paducah, Kentucky
Lone Oak News, 1996
Market House Museum
McCracken County Genealogical Society *History
    Of McCracken County,* Turner Publishing, 1989
Memorial Record of Western Kentucky, Lewis Publishing,
    Louisville
Neuman, Fred, *The Story of Paducah,* Young Printing, Paducah
    1927, revised by Catherine Neuman Adams, Image
    Graphics, 1979
Ninth Air Force Association Flyer, Navarre, Florida.
The Paducah Sun
The Paducah News Democrat
The Paducah Evening Sun
The Courier Journal, Louisville
The Commercial Appeal, Memphis
The Paducah Public Library, Microfilm and Microfiche.
Peoples Bank and Trust History, Ernest Walls, Turner Publishing,
    1988
Charity League Programs 1952-1956
Jaycee Minstrel Programs 1952,1953
Barbershopper Programs 1952,1953
Tennessee Valley Prospective 1975
Wells, Camille, *Architecture of Paducah and McCracken County*
    Image Graphics, 1981

My Paducah

Mail to:

Barrons Books
4704 Buckner Lane
Paducah, KY 42001-5332

For Orders Call: 270-443-1205

Email Orders: bwhitey@webtv.net

Please send me ___ copies of
    My Paducah   @ 19.95 each   _____
    Postage & handling*   _____
    Kentucky residents add 6% sales tax _____

Total enclosed _____

* Postage & handling charges - $5.00 for first book
                and $.50 for each additional

Make checks or money order to Barrons Books

Ship to:

NAME _____

ADDRESS _____

CITY _____ STATE ___ ZIP _____

Please Copy